101 THINGS

EVERY MAN

SHOULD KNOW

TO EXPERIENCE A LIFE

OF VICTORY & IMPACT

101 THINGS

EVERY MAN

SHOULD KNOW

TO EXPERIENCE A LIFE

OF VICTORY & IMPACT

DAK FREDERICK

101 Things Every Man Should Know
(To Experience a Life of Victory and Impact)
Copyright © Dak Frederick, 2021

ISBN: 978-0-578-95196-6

Library of Congress Control Number: 2021904191

Visit: www.habitsforgrowth.com/bonus101!

DEDICATION

To God:

At one point in my life, I wanted nothing to do with you. Despite my efforts to run away from you and live life on my own terms, you continued to pursue me. You had a plan to use my struggles, failures, and successes to be an encouragement to others. I acknowledge that everything I have is because of your mercy and grace. Thank you for not giving up on me.

To My Wife:

I know how much it meant for you to see me complete this book. You have been with me and seen this project evolve from the ground up. Thank you for all the extra time and energy you sacrificed to allow me to finish this book. You've been patient with me and have helped me to stay focused and clearheaded as I worked on this very important project. Without you, this book would not exist. Your prayers have carried me along this journey.

To My Mom:

Thank you for all your support and encouragement and for believing in me. This whole time you have spoken blessings into my life. You've given a lot to see your children succeed in life and it is not in vain.

CONTENTS

INTRODUCTION

This book will have the greatest impact on the man who's faced challenge and adversity, in a way that drove him to search for a better way of doing life. For the man who made a commitment to himself that he would never settle for a life of mediocrity. He's driven by a hunger to be a better man and knows there's too much on the line to live any other way.

I wrote this book for the man who needs to fight back against what's become common for so many men: a life that's dry, unfulfilling, and full of regrets about what they should have done, could have had, or should have been. This book offers hope, comfort, and direction for the man who still struggles from the effects of not having the type of father figure or role model to show him a better way of life. The man who will excel if he's pointed in the right direction.

It's for men like you, who work hard yet struggle quietly. There's a part of you no one knows about, except you and God, that if exposed, would reveal struggles like a lack of direction, feelings of inadequacy, and a desire to know what your purpose in life is. You want to reach your full potential but sometimes feel like something is holding you back.

It's for the man who has goals and dreams and needs a way to make them become reality. I want to see that man learn how to turn self-doubt into faith, overcome toxic thoughts, and develop habits that will help him become more productive and successful.

This book is also for the man who is at the edge of nearly losing everything, or even giving up on life itself. If you take the time to really explore the depth of information that I've poured into this book, I can almost promise you'll experience victory in many areas of your life.

As a Retired U.S. Marine, I've faced some of the most challenging physical, mental, and spiritual hardships anyone could ever experience. I've been tested at times to what felt like my limit. I'm simply a student of life who is diligent about reaching my fullest potential and helping those around me reach theirs.

Make the decision to do everything it takes to live a life of victory and impact—for you—and for the ones you love. Knowledge does absolutely nothing unless it's applied, so it's my hope that you will take what you read here and put it into action. I'm rooting for you!

Part One

MINDSET IS EVERYTHING

1

FACE THE WIND

My youngest daughter and I, along with a growing crowd of people at a local park, stood watching a man on top of a hill with a bright orange parachute strapped to his waist. He was trying to "catch wind" so he could eventually fly. We spent so much time watching as he miserably failed to take off. I wanted to just walk away but we'd already been there so long, I would hate to have missed it if he took flight.

After looking at my watch to see how much time passed, I shook my head, grabbed my daughter's hand, and started heading back toward the bike trail. That's when he finally started making progress. He got enough wind to pop open his parachute. But he did something I didn't expect. Instead of turning his back to the wind and allowing it to blow him across the sky, he turned directly toward the wind. Before he could take off, he needed to "face the wind."

Throughout this book, there will be times where I'll challenge you to "face the wind." There will be some hard conversations—not like the ones you hear in the barbershop or when you're hanging out with the fellas. That's because I know that for you to "take flight," you too will have to make an active decision to "face

17

the wind." I'll admit that some of what you read will be equally as hard for you to hear as it was for me to write. I wrote this book because I genuinely want to help you.

Reflection Questions

1. Are there tough area(s) in your life you've been avoiding, where you think you need to "face the wind?" (Example: a tough decision you've been putting off, a relationship that needs to be restored).

2. Are there areas where your progress is slower than you want it to be? If so, why? Are there any steps you need to take to start moving further along?

3. Do your daily activities reflect actions that move you closer to your goal of making an impact? If not, what types of things do you need to start including in your schedule?

2

THE EASY ROAD VS THE HARD ROAD

The path that seems the easiest to travel isn't always the best one to take. Sometimes victory only comes by taking the hard path. During my combat training in the Marines, I learned to never take the path that looks smooth. Picture two scenarios, one where there's a bunch of thick grass and brush, the other where there's a nice clear trail that takes almost no effort to cross. Which one sounds better? Naturally, it would seem like it makes sense to take the easier path.

The true difference between the two paths isn't what you see in the beginning, but what you see in the end. The easy path we were told, was the one the enemy has already traveled on. He's already had opportunities to set traps and is watching and hoping you'll travel down that path. They know human nature is to do what's most comfortable and easy.

On the other hand, the hard path is one the enemy hasn't traveled on, he doesn't expect you to take it, and when you approach him from a different angle, your chances of victory drastically increase. You decided to take a path most would never take, and as a result, you have a higher chance of victory. This way of thinking goes against what most people would ever tell you.

This type of mindset is the reason why when you even mention the word "Marines," there's a certain level of respect. They're known for their battlefield success. Unfortunately, many people who are capable of great feats who miss out because they choose the easy approach to life. They settle for being average, mediocre, and not going anywhere in life.

It doesn't take much effort to live like this. Here's what the easy path looks like in the beginning: eat whatever I want, don't work out, never spend time with your kids, spend what I don't have, say whatever I want, don't care how I use my time. When you're on the easy path, where does it eventually take you to?

Health problems that result from neglect, weight problems that could have been prevented, a poor relationship with your kids and missing out on opportunities to pour into their lives, hurt feelings and relationships that result from careless words, and eventually a life of regret because of the time you wasted that could have been spent doing something you can look back on and be proud of.

These are just a few examples of where the easy path will take you. Naturally, it might seem like the easier path, but when you choose the hard path, you will begin to stand out. When everything inside of you cries out to take the easy path that leads to mediocrity, make the decision to take the hard path that leads to victory.

If you do, you'll look back at your life and be glad you didn't take the easy way out because your life will be filled with victory and success, instead of regret. I want this for you, me, and future generations of men.

REFLECTION QUESTIONS

1. Take a look at your life. Have you been settling for the easy path?

2. Take a look at the people around you. What path are they on?

3. What does it mean to you to not be average or mediocre?

3

NOT MAKING THE PROGRESS YOU WANT IN LIFE?

Slow progress is better than no progress. Sometimes when you're working toward a goal it can seem like it's taking forever to get there. You might feel like the progress you're making isn't enough. I know how that feels. It took me 14 years to get a four-year degree.

In between military deployments, special duty assignments, and the responsibilities of having a family, I slipped in a class here or there, until I finally made it. Graduating and completing my bachelor's degree opened the door for me to get a high-paying job after leaving the military.

I had many years where I just wasted time and had no excuse for not going to college. I'm just glad I didn't allow the setbacks I experienced to keep me from pursuing my goal. The same thing applied to writing this book. Slow progress for me meant writing this book in small chunks. To start, all I had was a note saved on my phone. Anytime an idea came to my mind, I typed it and moved on with my day. It was this slow trickle of ideas, that over time eventually turned into this book.

If it feels like you're not making progress in life, it could be because you haven't been intentional enough about the direction you're headed in. I want to spend some time in the next chapter, helping you map out some direction for your life. It's important to read this next chapter because it will help you as you read the rest of this book. You'll be able to start setting some goals you can be more intentional about working toward.

4

THIS IS UGLY—BUT I'M DOING IT ANYWAY

After several rounds of getting knocked down, dragging himself back onto his feet, and back into his corner to get his bloody face patched up before returning into the ring, Rocky Balboa demonstrates the most important thing any of us could ever remember: the path to victory is often an ugly one. Most of us call that perseverance. If you expect to go anywhere in life, you have to be willing to do what's ugly—and keep doing it.

Have you ever had a goal you were excited about, but once you started working toward it, things didn't seem as great as they did when all you had was motivation and a goal (and a cup of coffee if you're a caffeine junkie)? I know what that's like. A few years ago, I started taking vocal lessons. My roots as a musician and singer go back as far as a young boy of eight years old. I signed up for band because I wanted to play the saxophone.

Instead, the teacher handed me a baritone—the instrument that's one step before the tuba. I did everything I could to try to play that thing but the best I could do was make *the worst sounds* known to mankind.

After that year of torturing my family—and myself, I decided to let go of the baritone and since then I *never* looked back. Eventually, I found my way toward the piano and clarinet. My experience with these instruments was much better. Fast-forwarding to over twenty years later, I decided to pay for professional voice training.

There's something my vocal teacher said during our first lesson I will always remember; "If you want to get better, you have to be okay making ugly sounds!" With my previous experience playing the baritone, this was the *last* thing I wanted to hear but over the next couple of years I embraced this concept of doing what was ugly.

Because I got used to doing what sounded ugly, I worked up the nerve to stand up in front of a crowd of hundreds of strangers at an opera dinner theater in Paris, so I could sing to my wife on our eighth wedding anniversary. Before I started this journey, I never thought I would ever be able to do something like this. Are you willing to do what's ugly to accomplish your goals?

That might mean picking up another job for a short time so you can get out of debt. It could mean doing something where you feel like a complete beginner, even though you might look bad because you're so unskilled at it. Whatever it might be for you, are you willing to do what feels ugly right now, and stick with it so you can experience new levels of success? If you are, you never know where you might end up at.

5

LOSING AND WINNING:
A LESSON IN HUMILITY

When I was in Marine Corps boot camp, we did pugil stick fighting—training we conducted using long, padded wooden sticks to simulate striking someone in the face and body with a rifle. I'd beaten a couple people in a row and had the confidence of Muhammad Ali. Then I squared up against a guy who was about 5'3." If laughing were allowed, I'm sure I would have let out a loud one. All I could think was: "This is going to be an easy win."

After the instructor sounded a loud whistle blow, we both approached the center of the fighting pit. Before I could even get one strike in, he hit me with several vertical and horizontal blows to the head and chest and knocked me to the ground. What at first was supposed to be an easy win for me, turned out to be a quick upset. I lost before I even had a chance to blink.

Maybe if I had a little more humility, I would have approached that fight with the same tenacity as the other ones. But I thought I was going to win because I was up against a smaller opponent. I underestimated his ability and overestimated my skill level. I was too prideful and needed to experience some humility to see the importance of not letting my guard down. If you're a Christian, realizing this is especially true for you too.

I can't even count how many times I've seen someone come running for help, to be rescued out of a tough situation they can't get themselves out of. They get the help they need and as soon as things start going well, you can't find them anywhere. If you try to give them advice, they shove it away and no longer need help from any of the people they were begging help from.

When things are good, they're "winning," and end up doing the same thing I did in that fight: they let their guard down. Then they experience a knockout and have to become humble again. It's easy to achieve success and then forget God is the One who gives you the ability to have what you have.

When you forget that, you become a prime candidate for a lesson in humility. I'm glad I lost that fight because it's a continual reminder I need to stay humble. Sometimes the greatest lessons in humility rise from the ashes of defeat.

REFLECTION QUESTIONS

1. Are there area(s) where you need to be more humble?
   (Ex: a tough decision you've been putting off, a relationship that needs to be restored)

2. What lessons in humility have you learned in your life?

3. Are you a better man today because of what you learned?

6

THE ONE THING YOU CAN'T
TAKE AWAY FROM ME

End each day knowing you did your best and kept your integrity. No matter what your paycheck looks like (big or small), no matter how many accolades you get (lots or very few), you can always be content at the end of the day knowing you did what was right.

After retiring from the Marines, I landed a job in the insurance industry. It was a job with great pay and benefits. They had designated rooms with recliners where you could go and take naps. We had free food all the time, lots of activities and games, several break rooms with big-screen televisions and beanie cushions to relax on. They treated us well. After a few months of working there, I noticed something strange.

At the end of the day, I was usually one of the few people still answering calls and working with clients. Out of hundreds of people, why were there only a handful of people who stayed behind handling clients on the phone? I figured out what was happening.

Since the company instructed us to keep our phone lines open until the end of our shift, those who followed the policy would pick up the phone even if it were the end of their shift and there was only a minute left. This sometimes meant staying on the phone for an hour past schedule.

On several occasions, I stayed late because I wanted to keep my integrity and do what I was hired to do. I love spending time with my wife and kids and I'm not the type of person to spend extra hours at work. On those days I went home knowing I kept my integrity. Did I agree with their policy? No—but they didn't hire me to agree with their policies—they hired me to take care of clients and that's what I did.

There's a universal law that you reap what you sow. After only a couple of months, I received a reward from our Investigations Unit for stopping two people who were in the middle of committing insurance fraud for thousands of dollars. My hard work was recognized, and it set me up for future opportunities to get promoted within the company.

I've had other times where it felt like it wasn't worth it to give my best because it was unappreciated, there was no reward, and it seemed like others were getting paid the same amount of money to do way less work. Sometimes it might seem like it's not worth it but keep at it. At the end of the day, you'll still have the one thing nobody can take away from you: your integrity.

7

YOU DON'T KNOW MY DAD: AVOIDING THE BLAME GAME

Just because you were fatherless, it doesn't mean you can't be prosperous. Sadly, there are a lot of men today who come from homes where there was no positive male role model present. Many of them never knew their fathers yet others had a dad who lived in the home who wasn't as involved as he could have been.

I understand the pain of having a dad who wasn't around like he should have been. You might have had a bad example in the past, but that's not an excuse for making bad decisions in the present. I know what it's like to see my dad struggle with drugs and alcohol, but I used that as fuel to live a better life and give more to my children than what he gave to me.

Yes, it's true your environment helps shape who you are, but it's also true your environment doesn't have the final say so. There are some incredible men we can look to as sources of inspiration who show that no matter your past, you don't have to accept a life of defeat and mediocrity. Do you find yourself stuck in the past and focused on what you didn't have growing up? No matter what your situation is, you can accept responsibility for the decisions you make now. The following exercise is for any man, not just those who come from fatherless homes. I believe his story is something all men need to hear.

REFLECTION EXERCISE

1. Watch Jim Daly's Inspirational story on YouTube on how he overcame resentment toward his abusive, alcoholic dad: "Redeeming Fatherhood When It's Broken."[1]

2. Describe any point(s) in his story you can relate to.

3. Write down why you believe no matter someone's situation, they can succeed in life.

8

THINKING THE NEXT MAN HAS IT BETTER THAN YOU

Stop thinking the next man has it better than you. He's probably thinking the same about you but will never admit it. One summer afternoon a red sports convertible that looked like it just pulled off the showroom floor pulls up to a stop sign.

The driver looks to his left and sees a man laughing and wrestling around with a little boy. Both men look up at each other at the same time and briefly exchange a cordial nod. The man driving the luxury car goes home to an empty house and thinks to himself how great of a life it would be to have a family of his own and be able to horse around with his son.

The man horsing around with his son wonders with intrigue what it must be like to live a lifestyle of luxury. He thinks to himself. "I wonder what it would be like to drive a nice convertible like that." If only I had that type of money." Both men are so focused on what the other one has that they're failing to realize the significance of their own blessings. Stop worrying about how much someone else has achieved or how far they've gone in life.

We each have our own journey and it will look different for everyone. The list of things you can compare yourself to someone else with is endless. Even on your worst day, the opportunities you have to thank God for what you have are also endless. Find ways to enjoy the blessings you have.

REFLECTION QUESTIONS

1. Do you find yourself comparing your life to those around you?

2. Can you name instances where you fell into the trap of thinking someone had it better off than you?

3. If so, how did it make you feel? Did it motivate you to do better or did it create feelings of insecurity and jealousy?

9

THE THINGS WE DO FOR APPROVAL

I'm just glad my mom was smart enough not to buy into the idea that getting other people's approval was worth spending money you didn't have. Growing up I got teased for wearing Pro Wing 2000's. If social media existed back then, I'm sure my shoes would have ended up going viral. I can just see it now: A bunch of emojis with laughing faces being posted all over the Internet of my Payless shoes.

Most of the kids I went to school with wouldn't have dared to wear anything other than Jordans, Reeboks, or some other name-brand shoe. Why? It was important to have approval from your classmates. Even more important, was not getting teased because you couldn't afford expensive shoes. What's ironic is not many of us could afford expensive name-brands.

My big day came. One day my dad bought me a pair of purple Reebok pump shoes from an outlet store. I was glad to finally have some name-brand shoes, but they were the ugliest pair of shoes I'd ever seen. Compared to my Reeboks, my Pro Wing 2000's were starting to look like a great option. Despite that, I decided to wear my new shoes to school anyway. One of my classmates stopped me to ask where I had gotten my new Reeboks from.

He was somebody who always had the latest brand names and

was usually the first person to tease me. That day was different though. He knelt and pumped my shoes a few times, walked around them like he was checking out a new sports car, and walked away like he had just seen a Lamborghini. For me, that was instant approval. I went from being the boy who was teased to getting respect. That day I went from hating my purple Reebok gym shoes to loving them.

For the first time, I understood why so many people were willing to spend hundreds of dollars on things they couldn't afford. Just like these kids, a lot of men still make decisions based on the need for approval. They will buy big houses and fancy cars they can't afford, just to gain the respect of their peers. Some will even spend top dollar to buy expensive clothing they can't afford.

If how you value your worth rises or falls on the approval you receive from others, you are selling yourself short. It's ridiculous to spend your life trying to gain other people's approval. Most of the people I went to school with, I'll never see. Most of the people you'll try to impress have their own issues. Don't waste your money or time.

Sometimes people make decisions that ruin their lives and hurt their families just so they can gain the approval of other people. Sometimes you will have to stare directly into the face of disapproval and make an unpopular decision because you know it's the right thing to do.

REFLECTION QUESTIONS

1. Name the people in your life whose opinions matter to you?

2. Describe situations where you have engaged in approval-seeking behavior.

3. Describe any changes you need to make when it comes to seeking the approval of others.

10

I'M RUNNING OUT OF BLESSINGS

Life is hard, and sometimes it's hard to be optimistic, even when you're trying your best to stay positive and be grateful. My wife is one of those rare women who can still cook and bake from scratch. She's one of the few people I know who doesn't make cornbread out of a box. One day, in our earlier years of marriage, she made breakfast for us.

It didn't take long before my face scrunched up and I had my finger in my mouth trying to figure out where the eggshell I was chewing was. She apologized and I said, that's okay I'm just glad I have food. I kept chewing and after a couple of minutes, it happened again. This time my wife apologized, and I said, that's okay at least I have a good wife and I'm able to sit here and eat breakfast with her.

Was that the last time it happened? Nope! I did my best to be grateful for my food, but by this point, I was tired of eating eggshells for breakfast. It happened again and she apologized. I said that's okay, at least there are other things on the plate that I'm able to enjoy. The fourth time it happened she apologized and instead of thinking about something positive to say, I told her "I'm running out of blessings!"

We had a good laugh for the day and continued with our meal. It's easy to hit points in life where you're trying to be grateful but when you look around, it seems like all you're doing is *chewing eggshells*. You can either choose to live every day complaining about eggshells or you can find things to be grateful for.

Something I've done before that helps me have a better outlook on life is what I call "thank you walks." This is where I take time and think about what I'm grateful for. I've done this by myself, but I've also done this with my wife. One time we spent a whole hour taking turns saying what we were grateful for while walking together.

There's something about doing this that always left us with a deep sense of gratitude. If you're stuck at a point in your life where you feel like things are just tough, try this out. Do a "thank you walk" or a "thank you drive." On your way to work, turn off the radio and just start thanking God for anything you can think of. The more you do this, the better your attitude will become.

It will help you not to forget that what you have today, isn't guaranteed to be what you have tomorrow. Life is precious but it's also fragile. The job you have today might be gone tomorrow. The health you enjoy today might be different tomorrow. The one you love most might not be here. Thank God every day for His blessings and provisions, no matter how you feel.

REFLECTION QUESTIONS

1. On a scale from 1-10, 1 being very ungrateful and 10 being extremely grateful, how would you say you rank in terms of being grateful for the blessings you have?

2. List 10 things you're grateful for.

3. Do a "thank you walk" or invite a friend to join you for a "thank you" session, where you just go back and forth and just say what you're grateful for.

11

PAY NOW, PLAY LATER

Pay now, play later. This has been my motto throughout much of my adulthood. It's up to you to choose whether you'll take life seriously today. I had a Sunday school teacher who once said, "A wasted life is a culmination of a bunch of wasted days." Like a lot of people I know, I found myself in my younger adult years wasting time, money, and energy on things that had no value.

I spent more money on alcohol than I care to admit. During those times I lived without a sense of purpose. After a while, I was miserable—even though I tried to pretend this lifestyle of partying and drinking was great. I was like a kid on a playground—so I thought. Growing up I always heard the adults say things like, "It's all fun and games until someone gets hurt." While I was playing around, my life was falling apart little by little. My "fun" and "games" left me depressed and in debt.

A playground was made for boys, a battlefield was made for men. I wish this part of the book were only for young twenty-year-old men, but sadly, some men reach well into their fifties and sixties and still haven't learned this lesson.

Your style of play might not leave you with a hangover in the morning like mine did, but regardless, you can choose whether you're going to slide your way through life, or if you're going to start getting serious. Don't get me wrong, all work and no play is not good for your health. But all play and no work is a child's mentality.

I like this quote by Brian Tracy: "The ability to discipline yourself to delay gratification in the short term to enjoy greater rewards in the long term, is the indispensable prerequisite for success." Which one will you choose? Play now, pay later, or pay now, play later? That's a decision only you can make.

REFLECTION QUESTIONS

1. I know I need to get more serious about (describe them).

2. The result of not getting serious about these things is (the people it will affect, the success I'll have, etc.).

3. I'm willing to delay gratification in the following areas so I can experience long-term success (describe them).

12

IF YOU NEED HELP YOU'RE WEAK

Needing help doesn't make you weak. The entire universe exists of symbiotic relationships—things working together to help each other—and so should you. Take the Nile crocodile, for example. It's known for being "hyper-aggressive whenever an uninvited visitor steps into their territory." Yet even this strong, tough-as-nails creature will allow a bird known as the "Crocodile Bird" to remove decomposing meat stuck between their teeth.[2]

I used to pride myself on not needing anyone else. I was determined to do life on my own without needing the help of others. I did this for so long, by the time I realized what I was doing, it felt nearly impossible to break that mindset. Don't sell yourself short of experiencing new friendships, getting help when you need it, or having a better quality of life.

Imagine that Crocodile with all that decomposed meat caked on its teeth. That's exactly what would have happened if he rejected any outside help. Don't allow yourself to walk around with a life that's slowly rotting away because you won't reach out and ask for the help you need.

REFLECTION QUESTIONS

1. Is there an area in your life where you need to ask for help?

2. What things are holding you back from getting the help you need?

3. What will happen if you never seek help?

13

QUIT SLACKING

Slacking off is somewhere between missing the game-winning shot and quitting the team altogether. You're still on the roster so it's not as easy for someone to say you quit, yet you're not doing much to help the team either. Let me just say this. I believe most of the men who read this book aren't in this category.

You didn't pick this book up because you're a slacker. Even so, there might still be areas of your life where you once were working hard and praying about but now you invest little time in. Sometimes even when you're giving the same amount of time to something your heart might not be in it; you can lack the same fire you once did. You don't go the extra mile like you used to.

That's like a business that has a grand opening, has great customer service, gives great deals, and then once they build up their clientele, they don't care as much. They change the recipe you fell in love with, the waiters look like they just had their wisdom teeth pulled, and your experience is nothing like what it was in the beginning.

You can be doing all the same things you normally do yet lack that fire you had in the beginning. You don't go the extra mile like you used to. You know what I'm talking about, especially if you're married. I'm guilty of this too. When you first start dating, you have all the time in the world for each other. You bought gifts and flowers all the time. You invested a lot into your relationship. Then you got married and start slacking off.

What about the guy who wants to make a great first impression on his new job and is putting his best foot forward? Then over time, you notice he's starting to come in late. He doesn't do anything more than what's required of him, and he barely does that sometimes. He's the guy no one can figure out why he hadn't been fired yet. He's the definition of a slacker. You have too much character to conduct yourself like that.

Even so, there might be areas in your personal and professional life you let slip. If you're not a habitual slacker but find yourself slipping toward that path, it's possible you just need to take a vacation from work and get recharged. Take care of yourself and do what you need to stay on track. The path to victory and impact is not for slackers.

14

TREAT FAILURE LIKE A GIFT

What happens when you pour your heart into something, and it falls apart? You hope things will turn out great but then they don't. That sounds like something most people can relate to. It's easy for someone to just say, "Just get back up and keep going."

It's not always that easy. Most of the time failure can seem like a curse, but you can experience your greatest blessing by treating your failure like a gift. That's exactly what Thomas Edison did. When he referred to his journey to creating a lightbulb that lasted 1,200 hours he said, "I have not failed. I've just found 10,000 ways that won't work."

I believe failure is a gift from God to protect you from the pitfall of becoming prideful and to cause you to become creative and find a different, better way of achieving your goal. Your response to failure will determine your level of victory and impact. Think about what happened to Thomas Edison.

His teacher considered him to be a complete academic failure and basically told him he was an idiot who was incapable of learning anything. I'm sure if she knew what he would turn out to be, she never would have said that. Then again, this was a classic example of how his failure at school led his mom to homeschool him, which led to his future success.

I like what Winston Churchill once said: "Success consists of going from failure to failure without loss of enthusiasm." Choose to live without regret over your failures. Learn from them and move on. Choose to live in victory. Use your failures to make a positive impact on others by helping them not make the same choices as you. Your failure can become someone else's gift if you'll allow it to be.

15

STOP THINKING YOU'RE NOT GOOD ENOUGH

How many times have you missed out on an opportunity because you thought something was too big for you? There was a career you thought about pursuing but weren't smart enough. There was a woman you wanted to ask out, but you didn't think she would be into you. You wanted to start a business, but you didn't think you had the skills to do it.

It seems like others around you are doing well but you're just stuck and eventually you think you're just supposed to be one of the people in the world who barely has anything, barely ever accomplishes anything, and never gets taken seriously. I can relate to these types of feelings. When I first realized I had a desire to write books to encourage people to reach their full potential, I had a lot of those "not good enough" thoughts.

I dealt with these same types of negative thoughts. "I'm young, who's going to listen to me." "I'm not rich, I don't have some super charismatic personality people just flock to and want to follow, I'm not flashy." "I'm not some brainiac with a super high IQ who can impress people with my presentation of intellectual arguments." Some call it the inner critic: that voice that every time you try to take a step forward or step out and do something big, that tells you you're just not good enough.

Each of us has a God-given path, but it's too easy to limit God before we even find out where He wants that path to lead to. I've found the things I'm most confident in my ability to do are the things that don't always turn out the best. It's usually through those times where I have these same thoughts of not being good enough that God shows me I don't have to be "good enough" to have and do what He purposes for my life.

I don't always "feel" like a good enough dad, or husband, or writer, but I don't let that hold me back from giving it all I have and trusting God to help me be and do more than I could ever imagine. Stop worrying about whether you're good enough, trust that God is good enough and that if He has called you to do something, He will give you what you need to accomplish it. Think big, pray big, expect big things to happen, and prepare like they will. Don't limit yourself and don't limit God.

16

STOP WORRYING ABOUT THEM

Do your part—trust God to do His—don't worry about who's not doing theirs. A few years ago, I took my daughters to an indoor play area inside of the mall. They quickly found some playmates and began running around, screaming, and doing what kids do best. They started racing each other and it didn't take long before I had my camera out filming my oldest daughter, who was the fastest one in the group.

I felt like I was watching an Olympic runner who left the competition in the dust. Just as I was starting to cheer her on, something I never expected happened. She looked backward while running forward. I didn't even see it coming because I was watching the screen on my smartphone while recording it; she ended running face-first into a wall.

What started as a victorious play time for my daughter ended up as a big mess. Fortunately, she didn't break any teeth or have to go to the emergency room. She learned a valuable lesson that day on why it's important to pay attention to what you're doing instead of looking back worrying about other people.

When you take your eyes off what you should be focused on and start looking around at what other people are doing, you could end up running into unnecessary obstacles: losing focus, slowing down, or just completely falling off track. Keep running your race, pay attention to doing your best, and you'll reap the rewards of your hard work. Stop worrying about them.

17

BE TEACHABLE

The military is a system of hierarchy that depends heavily on a rank structure. Typically, the people who are higher ranking are supposed to know more about life and their roles and responsibilities in the military. Unfortunately, sometimes people fall into the mentality that if someone's a newbie they don't know much.

I remember having a conversation with a Private First Class who had recently graduated boot camp. I found out he had a degree in biological psychology. He looked very young, and I would never have guessed he'd already been to college. Although I was several ranks higher than him, he taught me a lot of things I didn't know about how the brain responds to the stress of a combat environment.

When I was growing up it seemed like my dad always had an answer for every question I had. Now that I'm a dad I find myself falling into the trap of thinking I'm supposed to always know everything and have an answer. I know of a young man who heard about this book and said, "I don't think I need a book to tell me what a man should know. I already know 'cause I'm a man."

If you think you know everything then you will miss out on

discovering a lot of things. Make it a point to be teachable even if it's from someone who's younger, or in a lower position of authority or management than you. Many people say "Experience is the best teacher;" however, I believe other people's experiences are the best teacher. Continue to learn, grow, and share with those who are teachable, and you'll experience a rich and rewarding life.

18

THINK LIKE AN ARCHAEOLOGIST

Have you ever reached a point where you were working hard and putting all your effort into something you knew you were called to do, yet it didn't look like you would ever see any results? At some point, no matter who you are, how talented you are, or how many resources you have, if you're trying to live a life of victory and impact, things will feel the exact opposite.

Sometimes you might feel defeated and even wonder whether you're even on the right path. There are six things I believe we can learn from how an archaeologist has to approach his work to be successful.

1. There are obstacles you have to overcome during your search.

2. It's exciting because you're on a journey and you don't know exactly what will happen next.

3. It requires patience.

4. You won't get what you're searching for if you don't keep looking.

5. Don't get disheartened when you don't pick up a strong

signal. You might keep going yet still not see any sign of progress. That's okay. Keep going.

6.   The treasure makes the search worth it.

The stage in life you're in could very well be what you need to go through to be able to fulfill God's plan for your future, but you can embrace today's struggle and enjoy today's victories. Stay excited about the possibilities of tomorrow but rooted in the realities of today. Be patient with the process, even when it seems like the process isn't taking you anywhere.

There are people who walk up and down the beach for hours at a time with a metal detector, looking for some type of treasure. If you've ever seen them, they're not frustrated at the fact they hadn't found anything yet, they're patiently hopeful about the possibility of what remains to be found. Stay focused and stay encouraged!

Part Two

I WANT MORE OUT OF LIFE

19

START HAVING FUN AGAIN

When your alarm goes off in the morning, do you grunt, beat your alarm clock for waking you up, and proceed to drag yourself out of bed? Do you say things like, "Just another day, just another dollar?" If so, I'm sorry to tell you but it sounds like you've settled for a dry, boring, mundane life. If you have fallen into this cycle, it's time to find a hobby, learn a skill, pick a fight (no, don't pick a fight, just kidding).

Please. Do something out of the ordinary. Try a new food, build something. Anything. Please! Sometimes the job you currently have isn't what you really want to do. You might be stuck every day going to a job you hate but at least you can find something productive and healthy to keep you motivated.

Here are a few ideas and resources to help you get started. There are thousands of ideas and if you do some digging around, you can find something. If you can't be excited about your work, at least you can be excited about your life after work. If you're blessed to have both, congratulations!

Ideas and Resources to Overcome a Boring Life

■ **Take up Martial Arts**

Visit https://blackbeltwiki.com/martial-arts-styles and choose from one of the 180 different styles of martial arts listed.

■ **Buy a Rod and Go Fishing**

This website provides information on permits and licenses needed for each state for fishing. It also lists information on requirements to hunt legally.

https://www.reserveamerica.com/marketing.do?goto=%2Flicenses%2FHuntingAndFishingByState.html

■ **Try Building Something**

Here's an article that lists 20 projects for beginners to get you started. You can also just go to Lowe's or Home Depot and let someone know you would like to do a weekend project and see if they have any ideas:

https://www.familyhandyman.com/list/surprisingly-simple-woodworking-projects-for-beginners/

■ **Learn a New Skill**

Go to www.udemy.com and you will find over 100,000 online courses on several interesting subjects you can even start a business from by learning. Examples of some of the classes they offer are:

-Health & Fitness

-Photography

-Personal Finance

-Productivity

-Voice Training

-Piano/Guitar Lessons

-Entrepreneurship

-Home Improvement

-Building a Website

-French, Spanish, German, etc.

■ **Other Activities to Do**

Start painting art. Even if you have no idea what you're doing, go to a local park, and talk to people as they go by. Tell them you're new at painting but would like to try to paint a picture for them for free. You might get laughed at, but you also might get in some good laughs yourself. You might meet some new friends doing this. On top of that, you'll eventually get better at it. How could you possibly be bored with life if you do stuff like this? I'm just giving this to you as an idea, but I want you to think of some more creative ways you can make your life more fun. Go to https://drawpaintacademy.com/painting-for-beginners/

-Visit a National Park

-Do a Search to see what events are happening around your area

-Try out a New Sport

-Bike Riding

-Go Bowling

-Play Golf

-Buy a Telescope and Spend Time Enjoying and Learning about the Solar System

-Try Doing a Science Experiment

-Learn how to use a Bow and Arrow (it goes without saying, but of course make sure you're aiming in a safe direction)

-Take up Sign Language

-Buy a Harmonica and Watch YouTube Videos for Lessons

-Do Indoor Rock Wall Climbing

-Try Indoor Skydiving (Notice I didn't say outdoor skydiving: that's because I'm not going to recommend anything I'm not willing to do myself).

-Go Ziplining

REFLECTION QUESTIONS

1. On a scale from 1-10 how exciting is your life (1= Compared to my life, a turtle seems to be having more fun than I am; 10= If I were having any more fun, I would feel guilty).

1   2   3   4   5   6   7   8   9   10

2. What's holding you back from living a more exciting life?

3. Out of the things listed, which ones are you willing to try?

4. List other ideas you're ready to try.

20

I GOT BIG DREAMS

What little boy doesn't have big dreams? Plans to be a professional athlete, a firefighter who saves lives, a surgeon, a soldier, an architect, a missionary. Sometimes they dream things that are even impossible yet believe they could happen. As a young boy, I stood outside with my friend and said, "I can jump over that roof!"

Those were the words of a seven-year-old boy who saw nothing but limitless potential in life. In my heart, I was convinced I could jump over that roof. Just like you, I had to grow up; and just like you, I fight to not lose that ability to dream big. You can be a man who keeps dreaming or one who allows the realities of a hard and sometimes cold world to all but extinguish any hope of ever being, having, or doing anything great.

I hope you haven't reached a point where you've stopped having any big dreams. Where you've just gotten used to existing—seeing other people move ahead, while settling for the same old way of life day in and day out. Don't you want more?

I want to encourage you to spend some time doing the following reflection exercise, where you just write down your dreams. Nothing is too crazy. I want you to use this exercise to dream like that little boy you once were, who didn't know anything about limitations. Even if it's something that's physically or practically impossible, write it down. Is it something that would take a miracle to happen? Write that down too. Of course, you're grateful for the blessings you have today, but that doesn't mean you have to place limitations on yourself for what's possible tomorrow.

REFLECTION QUESTIONS

1. What would the best version of yourself look like (character, skills, health, etc.).

2. If you had the money to support any cause, which one would you support? How much money would you want to give?

3. Where would you like to travel?

4. What type of people do you want to be surrounded by?

5. Note: If there are dreams that don't fit into these categories, make note of those as well.

21

TURNING YOUR DREAMS INTO REALITY

Having a dream doesn't take much work, but seeing the dream become reality does. Here's what happens to a lot of people. Just like we did in the last chapter, they get themselves pumped up about all the possibilities that could happen, but never do anything about them.

"The way to get started is to quit talking and begin doing," is what Walt Disney said and I agree with that statement. There's one step I want to place in between that will increase your chances of success: you need to have a plan on how you will get there. It's not enough to just walk around with a bunch of ideas floating around in your head.

If five people sit down to have a business meeting and leave without writing down anything they discussed, there's a good chance if you asked them a month later what they talked about, they wouldn't be able to tell you. Why?

A lot happened since then. The same thing can happen to you too if you have dreams and goals and you never write them down. When life happens sometimes it's easy for your dreams to get shoved aside. Next thing you know, that business you wanted to start never happens. You're still out of shape, you're digging into your savings account each month, and you're not satisfied. It doesn't have to be this way.

I want to use this section to help you write down your goals and make a bridge between your dreams and accomplishing them. In the next chapter, we're going to talk about why you should create a vision board. But for now, think about this: imagine hiring a company to build your dream home.

The carpenters, electricians, and other key players meet with the architect to discuss the building plans. The architect has all the ideas in his head, but no one writes them down or creates a digital format where they can be referenced later. They leave the meeting excited about the possibility of building this house. A day after they start building, a storm comes through and puts a stop to their work for an entire week.

Once they return, everyone begins working together. They each have an idea of the plan and it looks like they're moving in the right direction. Finally, they finish, and you get to see your newly built dream home. How come it doesn't look anything like you envisioned? You told them what you'd like to see, they had a bunch of people working toward it, and everyone knew the plan.

A lot of activity took place, but obviously, something was missing. That sounds like what I've done sometimes too. I start working toward something and in the end, it doesn't turn out as good as it should have been because I failed to map out my vision. I don't want that to happen to you. I've included the following reflection exercise, along with an article to help give you a good starting place.

REFLECTION EXERCISE (OPTIONAL)

1. Before you start this exercise make sure to gather the list of dreams you wrote down in the last chapter. If you didn't complete that exercise, go back, and take the time to do it now.

2. As pointed out in the tutorial video, A Complete Guide to Goal Setting, "People without goals are not as successful as they hope to be. People who don't write down goals are less likely to accomplish them."[3] In my opinion, this tutorial is excellent because it uses a lot of visual illustrations and breaks down a simple process for goal-setting. Are you going to take action?

22

THE POWER OF A VISION BOARD

Your outlook affects your outcome. A boy named Glenn Cunningham almost lost his life in a fire that started when he and his brother were trying to carry out their responsibility of filling up the kerosene heaters that kept their school warm.

The doctors told his parents that he would never walk again and that there was a chance his legs might have to be amputated. Glenn went from barely having any flesh on his bones, to setting a world record for the one-mile race, finishing it in 4:06.7.[4]

What makes his story so powerful is that while most saw him as just a crippled kid who would never walk again, he never accepted that as his fate. His vision of who he saw himself becoming and what he could do was strong. How many people in his situation would have the vision to see beyond their present situation?

You will eventually have, do, and become what your mind focuses on most. Ever notice how if you hear a song over and over, you start humming it without even trying to? Since you were repeatedly exposed to that song, your brain connected significance to it and kept bringing it to your mind.

A vision board will serve a similar purpose for you, except what you'll have is a way to train your brain to keep reminding you of your goals. I was first introduced to this concept in college, but I've used it in my personal life, and I believe it's a powerful tool. A vision board can be as simple as a poster board with a bunch of pictures cut out from magazines that help depict the goals and vision you have for your life.

When I was in college, I made a vision board that had a picture of a tassel, along with the name of my college and a sign that said, Congratulations, Class of 2018. I did the same type of thing for all the other goals I had for that year. One of the other things on my vision board was to become an author.

I created a small pamphlet before writing this book, but it was far from anything I could pin the title author next to. If you're reading this book, then you're part of the vision I saw three years ago. My goal didn't happen right away, but eventually it did. It was more motivating to walk by my vision board and see what direction I was headed in and what I was working so hard for.

Plus, it was a lot faster than trying to read through a list of goals every day. I want to encourage you to invest in your success by taking the time to create a vision board. Make it something fun that you do with your friends and family. Get some people on board and use a vision board to help you become more intentional about achieving your goals.

REFLECTION EXERCISE

1. Set a date and time to work on your vision board.

2. Gather up all your written dreams and motivational goal statements.

3. There's an article on Wikihow that's well-written and gives some excellent ideas on how to create your vision board. They give tips on how to choose the best format, find inspirational images, how to make the best use of your vision board, and a bunch of other things that could help you.[5]

23

HALF-TIME

What's the one thing most sports have in common? They have a half-time or some other period where the competitors rest and take a break. As a man, the only time someone will ever tell you to take a "half-time" is if you play a sport or your doctor places you on bedrest. Outside of that, you're going to have to take the initiative to plan these breaks yourself. If you don't, eventually you will experience burnout, "exhaustion of physical or emotional strength or motivation usually as a result of prolonged stress or frustration."[6]

A stressful lifestyle can put people under extreme pressure, to the point that they feel exhausted, empty, burned out, and unable to cope. Stress at work can also cause physical and mental symptoms. Possible causes include feeling either permanently overworked or under-challenged, being under time pressure, or having conflicts with colleagues. Extreme commitment that results in people neglecting their own needs may also be at the root of it. Problems caused by stress at work are a common reason for taking sick leave.[7]

If you had a favorite sports team and they were losing, which would you prefer: for the game to continue with no half-time or for them to take a break, go to the locker room get rested and refocused, and return with a new strategy and a new passion for winning? Of course, you want them to take a break so they will have the best chance for success.

Why not do the same for yourself? Plan regular times where you can get away from your normal responsibilities and get refocused. This is something I've started doing monthly. I plan what I call prayer retreats, where I spend an afternoon alone taking a walk, doing a workout, listening to my favorite music, praying, doing Bible studies, enjoying the outdoors, and just thinking about all the things I'm grateful for.

Each time I do this, I come back home feeling refreshed. Imagine an NBA player who plays all four quarters and never gets a half-time break. He's in the game the entire time giving everything he can. Even if he can manage doing this for one game, how long do you think that will last?

I've had those times where I experienced burnout from doing so much and not getting a break, that I eventually couldn't give 100% to any of the things I was doing. I'm not a fan of that and if that's what you're used to, I want to encourage you to take a half-time.

24

THE STOPWATCH METHOD

In the previous chapters you went through the process of dreaming again like you did when you were a kid. You made goals, put together a written plan, and even made a vision board to give you some daily motivation to help you stay on track. Just having goals and even writing them down is a big part of setting yourself up for success.

But doing all these things still doesn't guarantee you'll experience daily success. Because of that, I want to share with you something simple I do all the time. I've made progress in a lot of areas because of it. It's what I call the stopwatch method. To make the stopwatch method effective, at the beginning of the week, I estimate how much time I want to spend on different activities that week.

There are several ways I use this method. If I have to force myself to do something I don't want to do, I'll set my stopwatch and make myself do it until the time has ended. Sometimes by then, I'm motivated to keep going and I end up doing more than I intended to.

I use it for other things, like when I want to squeeze in a quick five-minute workout where I rotate between exercises every thirty seconds to one minute. If you have a smartphone, you probably have a timer. It's something you don't have to pay anything extra for. Use it to your advantage. In the next chapter, I'm going to discuss what's known as micro-habits. I'll explain how you can combine it with the stopwatch method to get a lot accomplished each day. Keeping track of your time will help you get a lot more accomplished.

25

SMALL HABITS, BIG WINS

Small habits lead to big wins. I've discovered that sometimes you can get a lot more done in five minutes of focused effort than thirty-five minutes of distracted work. If you're trying to develop a new skill or habit, combine the stopwatch method discussed in the previous chapter, with what's known as a micro-habit.

This is when you set a small goal that can easily be completed. When you do this, you prevent yourself from losing motivation, especially when it comes to things you don't want to do, but you're trying to force yourself to do anyway.[8] Last year I decided to start practicing the piano more consistently. I got tired of being hit-and-miss, so I set a goal of practicing five days a week for five minutes each time.

I set my stopwatch and once that time was up, I stopped—even if I had the time to keep going and wanted to continue. I did this for a while and eventually five minutes turned into thirty minutes. I had days where I practiced for an hour or more. This reminds me of a technique in weightlifting known as priming.

You start by doing extremely light weight and low reps. After doing this for two weeks your muscles will be screaming to lift something heavier. Picture somebody grabbing the back of your shirt while you're trying to break free from them. You have a lot of energy bound up that isn't going anywhere, but the minute they let you go, you fly forward.

Once you start adding that extra weight, you'll be surprised at how much easier it seems to lift. When you use micro-habits, you're setting yourself up to make big progress. Using the stopwatch method along with micro-habits is a great way to reach your goals. I included the following exercise to help you get started.

For now, just choose one or two things and commit to doing them consistently for one month. You can use this in your personal life, at work, or to start learning a new skill. Be creative and have fun reaching your goals.

SMALL HABITS, BIG WINS!

The purpose of this exercise to help you get specific about the amount of time you want to spend on different activities. Use the stopwatch method, combined with micro-habits to help you reach your goals. Grab a sheet of paper and make and use the format below to get started.

Activity/Project	Time Planned	#Times/Week
Example: Push-ups	1 Minute	5
Example: Reading	3 Minute	3

26

FOCUS ON THE MOST
IMPORTANT THINGS FIRST

One of the keys to being more productive is being able to focus your energy on the most important things first. I take this principle from the self-defense system known as Krav Maga, where the first step in any situation is to remove the immediate threat.

This means you deal with what poses the greatest consequence to you right now. If you're about to get attacked by three guys, you're going to focus your effort on the one who poses the greatest immediate risk to you. Get used to doing the most important things first—the things that if you leave undone, will cause you the greatest pain.

We have all dealt with the pain of not focusing on the most important things first. I know I have. I've stayed up late trying to finish a college paper that was 30% of my total grade because I failed to make it a priority like I should have. If you're trying to live a life of victory and impact, you'll have to learn how to pay attention to the things you do every day, and constantly ask yourself whether you're focusing on the most important things first.

REFLECTION QUESTIONS

1. Right now, what are some of the biggest challenges in your life that you need to focus on before they negatively impact you?

2. What are the positive things you can spend more time focusing on that will have the greatest level of impact?

27

KNOWING WHEN TO STOP

Sometimes the best action is to *stop* taking action. There have been times I've tried fixing something around the house and things didn't turn out the way I wanted. Like the time I was trying to fix the towel rack and ended up making an even bigger hole.

Then moved on to making other holes to try to fix the ones I messed up. There came a time where I just had to stop, or else there wouldn't have been a wall left to hang a towel rack on. Sometimes you just gotta know when it's time to move on. Just give it your best shot before you do.

When you have a goal you want to accomplish and you're determined to get it done, sometimes it's easy to get so focused on accomplishing the goal, that you forget why you set the goal in the first place. I remember when I was convinced that if I started reading a book, I had to finish it.

Most of the reading I do is for educational purposes but there have been times where I decided not to finish a book because I wasn't getting anything out of it. Recognize when you need to stop and move on to something better and more productive. Sometimes the best action is to *stop* taking action.

28

PREPARE AND KEEP YOUR SANITY

One of the best things you can do to be more productive is to do weekly and daily prep. A habit I've developed is looking at my calendar at the beginning of the week and seeing what needs to be done. I'll look over what goals I want to accomplish for that week and decide which days would be best to work on them.

I try to find ways to group activities that are in the same general area to avoid having to make multiple trips when necessary. Then my wife and I will talk through our week to see if we need to make any changes. From there I have a general idea of what my week would look like.

I'm not always the best at checking my schedule at night but I usually check it in the morning to see if there's anything I need to change. One thing that makes this process easier is that I've already decided how much time I want to spend on each day's activities. I've learned that even with a good plan, things can quickly fall apart if you forget about the little things.

That's why it's important to do things like prepping your lunch for the next day, making sure your clothes are ready, your gym bag is packed, etc. I know this sounds simple, but you'd be surprised how many people don't do this and end up frustrated because they're rushing everywhere or stressed out because they weren't prepared.

If you find that you're constantly forgetting things, buy a pack of post-it notes, write down things you want to make sure to remember in the morning, and place them next to your keys. Just make sure to place the note somewhere you'll see it. Prepare and keep your sanity.

29

PLANNING YOURSELF TO FAILURE

You can plan yourself to the point of failure. Some men are visionaries and have great dreams and intellect yet look back over their lives only to see a bunch of empty trails they mapped out in their minds but never stepped foot on. All plan and no action is worse than failure; at least if you fail you tried.

I think the tendency to over plan is a deep-seated fear of failure. At other times, it might just be a lack of organizational skills to put your plans into a logical sequence. It could be a lack of knowledge of how to turn your plans into reality. Whatever it might be, don't let years pass you by and you're still talking about the same thing you kept saying you were going to do ten, twenty years ago. Nobody takes you seriously anymore when you tell them what you're going to do. I've been there.

During my time in the Marines, I led a rifle detail that conducted burial services to honor veterans who passed away. As part of the service, three shots are fired into the air, which symbolizes the fact that we have properly taken care of one of our own (there's a lot more history behind this but I won't go into a lot of detail here).

Imagine how it would have looked for me to give the command, "Ready, Aim, Fire," and those three Marines in Dress Blues went through the motions—brought their rifle up their cheek like they were going to fire it but just stood there. That would be ridiculous. How ridiculous is it when you go through the motions, make everybody think you're going to do something, yet it never happens? There's no point in fooling yourself.

Dr. Henry Cloud said in his book, *Integrity*, about people who are forever stuck in a state of "Ready, Ready, Ready."[9] They plan and do so much talking that they never actually do anything. This could be starting a business, making a moving to another state, switching careers, or making a hard decision you know you should make. Whatever it is, don't let the enemy of over-planning and perfectionism stop you. I've done this too many times and still struggle to make this a thing of the past.

30

THE DIFFERENCE BETWEEN EFFORT AND EFFECTIVENESS

When I worked in recruiting, I would always hear: "Don't confuse effort with effectiveness." They wanted us to see that just because we were doing a lot of work, it didn't necessarily mean we were getting a lot accomplished. It's easy to get caught up doing busywork that doesn't move you any closer to your goals.

When you do this, you're wasting energy and won't have much to show for it. I first learned this lesson as a high school athlete. It was my first cross-country race and I stood at the starting line with probably a hundred other runners. All I could think about was that I needed to outrun every person out there.

That's exactly what I did. After the starting gunshot rang through the air, I took what was probably a 100-yard lead in front of a couple hundred runners. After a while, every few seconds a group of runners would run right past me. It got so bad, I thought I was going to finish in last place. What happened? I was expending a lot of energy, but my efforts weren't effective. I needed to change my method.

Eventually, I got to the point where I ran a 19-minute three-mile, but I had to learn that just because I was exerting a lot of energy, it didn't mean I was reaching my goal any faster or better. I had to learn to use my energy effectively. One of the biggest killers of productivity is focusing on things that won't get you to your goal.

This is something I battle with and have to constantly remind myself of. I have a mentor who suggested that when I'm trying to make decisions on how to use my time and conduct business, I should ask the question, "Is this the most important thing I should be doing right now?" Doing that has helped me learn how to shift my attention toward the things that will be the most effective.

31

THE RULE OF 3'S

The reason a lot of people don't accomplish their goals is that they're not able to link their *vision* with their daily actions.[10] This is one of the biggest things I've struggled with over the years. I experienced anxiety from not being focused and feeling like I never had enough time for what I desired to do. The problem wasn't with my time, it was with my intentionality. It's still a challenge, but I found a great way to help combat this.

I call it the 'Rule of 3's." This idea was inspired by a "Lead to Win" podcast episode.[11] Let me explain my process. At the beginning of the year, I decide what areas I want to set goals for: spiritual, relationship, financial, health, education, and business/work, etc. Next, I'll set one to three goals for each of those areas (or categories). Next, I break my year into quarters using 3's: January through March, April through June, July through September, and October through December.

At the beginning of each quarter, I look back on the progress I made for the previous quarter. Then I set one goal for each category that I'd like to accomplish in the next three months. After that, to reach those goals, I set which tasks are my top three priorities for each month. Then I break them down into weekly goals and tasks. After that, I focus on the top three tasks for each day. It's easier to stay focused this way because you can see how one simple task you do today directly links to a goal you want to accomplish for that week, month, quarter, and year.

If you approach planning this way, you'll be able to cut through all the distractions and focus on the tasks that will move you closer to your goals. If you would like me to walk you through my process, just shoot me an email at: dak@habitsforgrowth.com. I'd be more than glad to help you.

In the chapter titled "Turning Your Dreams into Reality," I gave you some ideas, along with a helpful resource to help you create a written plan for your dreams and goals. If you haven't already written down your dreams and gone through the process of putting deep thought and prayer into this, please go back to that chapter as well as the one titled "I Got Big Dreams." If you continue to apply the rule of 3's, it will help you simplify your life and stay focused on your most important goals and tasks.

32

BE SELECTIVE

If you want to live a life of victory and impact, you'll have to be selective. But what happens when you're not? You end up having friends who drag you down instead of lifting you up. You listen to news that stresses you out, leaves you in fear and anxiety, and surround yourself with people who never have anything positive to say.

You end up spending a lot of time and energy investing in people who don't want to grow. In some cases, people end up jumping into marriage out of desperation or just wanting to have a companion, then end up regretting their decision. It would be better for people to think you were crazy because you're selective about who you hang around, where you go, and the influences you allow in your life, than for you to just live haphazardly.

Charlie "Tremendous" Jones once said, "You will be the same person in five years as you are today except for the people you meet and the books you read [the places you go, the ideas you entertain, and the people you put your time and energy into]." I agree; choose wisely and be selective.

Part Three

PEOPLE: THE GOOD, THE BAD, THE UGLY

33

YOUR PRESENCE IS WORTH
MORE THAN YOU REALIZE

Being present is something you have to be intentional about, especially when you have a family. Sometimes after spending a hard day at work and dealing with some of the crazy things you might come across, the only thing you feel like you can give is your presence—and even doing that might feel difficult. But never underestimate how much of a difference just your presence can make in the lives of those around you. This is true especially if you have children at home.

There were times I was so tired all I could do was just sit there and let my daughters hang on my neck, squish my face together, and pull my arm. For them it was fun; for me, it took every bit of energy I had to be there for them. Sometimes you might not feel like being around because you're tired or you have a lot on your mind, but when you make a conscious decision to be present, you're making the first step in the right direction to being able to make the type of impact that will make a difference.

It might not always come naturally. I'll cover this in more detail in a later section, but, unfortunately, sometimes people can reach a point where they don't even know if anybody cares whether they're alive or not. I'm here to tell you that your presence matters more than you could ever know. My dad reached that point before I was born. His first child was killed by a drunk driver who was driving an 18-wheeler.

After this happened my dad went through such a dark period that he was seriously considering taking his life. That's when my mom told him that she was pregnant. He decided that it was worth sticking around to see his new child born into the world. I'm glad he made the right choice. The bottom line is that people need people. Your presence means more than you might ever realize.

34

BRINGING OUT THE BEST IN OTHERS

Sometimes it's easier to see the things that are wrong than it is the things that are right. Many people have jobs that train and require them to look for things that are out of place. A lifeguard trains to quickly notice when something has gone wrong. A doctor reading an x-ray needs to know when something is not right. Being able to spot things that are wrong or out of place is a necessary part of life.

Once I graduated Marine Corps boot camp I took leave and came home for a few days. One morning I decided to pull the microwave forward to check for dust. My mom always kept a clean house and tried to teach us to do the same, but I was a new person now.

Somehow before I left for boot camp I had trouble picking up after myself, now I was inspecting my house to see if it met the standards of cleanliness I'd been trained to keep. I called my mom over and said, "Mom, look, you see all this dust?" Her response: "Boy—you serious?" I was, but all she could do was smile. I'd been trained to not only spot things that are wrong but to actively look for them.

What about when it comes to people? Have you taken this approach of looking for flaws in others that you find it hard to think or say anything positive? When you make a conscious effort to focus on people's strengths rather than their weaknesses, they will sense that. They will know that you value them even though they don't "have it all together." You will meet people who have been told—in so many words—they're useless failures who won't amount to much.

I hope you haven't been the person to receive this type of treatment. I also hope that if you are the one dishing out the poison of negativity to those you live with, work with, and should be pouring into, that you decide to turn things around. Choose to focus on bringing out the best in others, not "moving the microwave to look for dust." Let people know you value them, look for their strengths and highlight them, and make a conscious effort to encourage others.

35

A POOR EXCUSE FOR
NOT STAYING IN TOUCH

Being busy is a poor excuse for not staying in touch with friends and relatives. It doesn't take much to make somebody's day. While I was still working on this book, a friend of mine who lives in Japan called me. That said a lot to me. This is someone who has a family with tons of responsibility, yet he took the time out of his day to call me.

When things like that happen, it feels good. The sad truth that I've heard so many people say over the years is, "why do we have to wait until somebody dies for us to take time for each other?" I wish it weren't like that but it's something I've experienced and been guilty of over the years.

I've seen social media posts where people were pleading with others to spend time with their families. You've probably seen them: posts that say things like, "If you have time to check your Instagram account, you have time to call your mom."

I wholeheartedly agree with that statement, yet sometimes I still find it challenging to keep in contact with my family like I should sometimes like I should. Learn to develop the habit of sending a text message, email, chat, or something that shows you're thinking about the people in your life who matter. I've tried all kinds of things to stay in touch with family: writing letters, creating reminders on my phone, printing out spreadsheets that have a date and time for me to make sure I contacted each person. I included a simple format you can use to make your own plan to help you stay committed to keeping in contact with your family and friends.

REFLECTION EXERCISE

Instructions: Grab a sheet of paper and list everyone you would want to stay in contact with. Post it in a place where you'll see it regularly. Make reminders on your phone. Do whatever you need to. Life is short and tomorrow is not promised.

Name	How Often to Contact	Next Scheduled Time
Example	Every Friday 5 pm	3rd Friday of May

36

SLAMMING THE BRAKES

How you "react," says much more about you than how you "act." I once had a coworker who was frustrated about how the person behind her was driving. In response, she slammed on her brakes and was rear-ended. She put several people's lives in danger and even messed up her car. She's got a whole different set of problems I won't even get into. She slammed the brakes on her car, but she should have slammed the brakes on her anger.

When you're frustrated and you have that text message, email, or social media post typed up and you're about to hit the send or post button, slam the brakes and don't do it. There's a good chance you won't regret your decision to hold off on sending your anger and frustration through the airwaves.

When we were still in high school, I had a friend whose dad ordered a burger. When they handed him his food, he checked to see if they made it the way he wanted to. He threw the burger back across the counter and told them to make it again. My friend's dad wasn't the type of person who was aggressive.

He didn't go around trying to intimidate people. He was a nice guy who was usually easy-going. But for some reason, this day he failed to slam the brakes. Every day you'll have opportunities to slam your brakes instead of going full force and using your strength to lash out in anger. Like my friend's dad, we're all humans and will mess up sometimes, but if you're going to be victorious your life can't be marked by anger.

The next time you want to lash out at someone, stop and think about how you can correct the situation. A little mercy goes a long way. Sometimes people will mess up. They will get the job wrong and sometimes it's frustrating when that happens. It's easy to take out your frustrations on the person behind the counter who messed up your order. It's easy to make someone feel like they're a failure because they didn't get it right.

We're all humans and will mess up. The next time you want to lash out at someone for their mistake, stop and think about what the best approach would be to help them correct the situation. Dale Carnegie said it this way: "If you want to gather honey, don't kick over the beehive."

In other words, if you resort to destructive, excessive means to try to get what you want, all that's going to happen is it will backfire on you. It might even seem like you're getting what you want right now, but eventually you won't like the result. Choose to "slam the brakes" and show mercy when you're angry or frustrated.

37

DON'T HOG THE SPOTLIGHT

Step back and let another man enjoy his moment in the spotlight. The men I've come to respect the most weren't the ones who always had to make sure everyone knew what their credentials were. I've observed that the men who have the biggest credentials behind them are usually the ones who have the smallest need to publicize their success.

On the opposite end, the guys who have done the least are often the ones who brag the most about what they've accomplished. This type of behavior stems from a need to feel respected, which all men have. I just want to highlight something I think is important.

Let's say someone's excited because they just completed their associate degree. They're getting compliments and they're happy about what they've accomplished. If you hold a Doctorate, find another time to talk about it. Don't hog the spotlight. Let another man have his moment of glory. It's only human nature to want to share your successes.

I've been in a lot of conversations where someone was bragging about their accomplishments, and it could have put a shadow on their excitement if I would have started bragging about what I've done. I think it's better to keep my mouth shut and let them enjoy their moment of fame. I try to do this, especially if they're sharing their success in front of a group of people.

I don't want to *one-up* another guy and take his moment away from him. You might have a better job, more degrees, leadership experience, or travel places those around you have never experienced, but the time to highlight that isn't while someone's in the middle of celebrating his success. Let another man enjoy his moment of glory. It won't cost you anything.

38

THE TYPE OF PEOPLE TO INVEST IN

I have adopted the principle of helping those who are trying to help themselves. For example, if there's somebody who needs to borrow some money, one of the things I consider is their spending habits. What's their lifestyle like? Are they trying to help themselves or are they looking for a handout? A couple of years ago, I was standing in line at the store when the lady in front of me didn't have enough to pay for her groceries.

Her cart was mostly junk food: candy, snacks, and sugary cereal. The cashier gave her the option to put one or two items back. Instead of the lady putting back some of her items and paying for what she could afford, she told the cashier to hold on for a second, held up a box of cereal and bag of cookies, and asked me if I would pay for them.

I'm sorry but I just couldn't get myself to pay for her groceries; I respectfully declined. She rolled her eyes at me and asked the person behind me to pay for her groceries. I'm all about giving and helping people, but she fell into the category of someone who's probably *not* trying to help themselves.

If she were responsible, she would have put something back, and she certainly wouldn't have held up the line asking people to pay for her snacks. She didn't seem like someone who was trying to help herself. You might have some of these types of people in your life.

Investing in people who don't want to help themselves is like trying to pour water into a covered glass. You could have taken that water, poured it into an open glass, and avoided wasting a valuable resource. Your time, money, and energy are all valuable. Don't waste them on people or projects that are dead.

This doesn't mean that you don't put effort into helping; it just means you know when to pull back your efforts. Sometimes the people you're trying to help will only sense the need to change when they sense the pain of not changing. That's hard to think about, especially when it comes to people you love.

This same thing can happen if you're a leader of a group of any kind. You can get trapped spending 90% of your time with the 10% of people who are causing the most problems. Invest in the right people but don't be too quick to judge. Sometimes the people who seem like they're the most promising are the ones who end up not doing anything, while the ones who seem the least likely end up doing the best. Invest in the right type of people and you will be glad you did.

39

YOU NEED LOYAL AND GENUINE FRIENDS

I'd rather have two loyal and genuine friends, than two hundred temporary and superficial friends. One of the most impactful decisions you'll ever make is who you surround yourself with. You want the type of people who will pick you up when you're falling, root with you when you're winning, and tell you the truth when you're slipping.

Too many men suffer because they don't have these kinds of friendships. I can't even count the number of conversations I've had with guys who failed to build these types of relationships. I've suffered in the past, believing things like, "I have no friends, nobody cares, it's just me out here on my own, no one cares enough to call me, the only time some people call me is when they need something."

If you're stuck in this place bro, don't stay here. You'll just keep going downhill mentally. I've been there and sometimes still find myself drifting back into that way of thinking. I consider myself blessed because I have the type of friends who call right when I need them and always have something positive to say. I have the type of friends I can talk about my struggles with, who encourage me and always point me in the right direction.

Even so, I've often failed to establish friendships like I should. Don't miss out on opportunities for friendship. Read through the ideas in the chapter titled, "Start Having Fun Again." Invite somebody to try some of those activities and go from there. In the chapter titled, "A Poor Excuse for Not Staying in Touch," I created a reflection exercise that will help you stay in touch with family and friends.

Use those questions to plan out some of the activities you'll do with someone and make sure to keep some good friends around. Friendship is a two-way street. You need friends who when you achieve success, they won't get quiet on you; they'll be the first ones to give you a fist bump and congratulate you.

You need the type of friends that when you're about to do or say something out of line, will be honest and have enough sense themselves to correct you. The type of friends, that when something tragic is happening in your life they will be there for you. I have a friend like this: my brother-in-law, Kenneth.

When he heard my mom was in the hospital dying, he fasted for an entire 48-hour period for her healing and recovery. How many people do you know would care enough to pass up food for two whole days, just to beg God to keep your mom alive? Thankfully, his prayers were answered. I've had times in my life where he's cared enough to speak up when he saw I was not headed in the right direction. He's what I call a loyal and genuine friend.

40

PEOPLE VIBE OFF YOU

People vibe off you, especially those you love most. As much as I try not to allow it to happen, when I walk into the house, sometimes the look on my face says, "I'm irritated right now, don't talk to me, just leave me alone." I fail to realize how big of an impact my mood has on those around me.

I might have allowed myself to get irritated about something or I'm not being grateful like I should be. At other times I allow somebody else's bad attitude or actions to cause me to get in a bad mood. We'll get to the section on marriage tips later in the book but here's a little tip.

I've heard it said you can tell a lot about a man by looking at his woman. I believe that a lot of times the look on a woman's face is a result of how her husband treats her. If he doesn't make her feel special and is always critical, it will show up in how she carries herself. She'll just look unhappy and unnourished, like a flower that's withering away. That's because he's sucking the life out of her.

On the other hand, a woman whose husband is showering her with love will usually respond by having a better attitude. She won't have that cold, hard, unemotional look that says, "I'm neglected. I need attention. I'm hurting." Then there are people like my youngest daughter who we call "Sunshine."

When she walks into a room, she automatically brightens it up with her cheerful personality. There are people in my neighborhood, who when I first moved in never waved at me. As I was on the way home from work or leaving to go somewhere I'd wave to them, and they'd just stand there with blank looks on their faces—I still don't get that but whatever. Over time I just continued to wave at them even though many times they never returned the favor.

Most of them now wave, but there's still one that I'm working on. I kept showing them kindness and in return, they eventually got the point and started doing the same thing. If I were still in my twenties before I became a Christian, I probably would have wanted to fight each time I waved at someone, and they didn't wave back.

Now I'm called to be a light for Christ and to show his love to the world. In what ways do people vibe off you? Are you cold, dead, and lifeless, or do your actions, words, and demeanor bring life and value to others?

41

I'M SORRY I HURT YOU

L earn to say sorry. At times this can be the toughest five-letter word in the English language. Never be in too high of a position, whether you have the status of a military General or CEO of a company. People will respect genuine remorse far more than excuses and cover-ups.

Sometimes you can make decisions that leave you and those around you busted and broken. If you've made a mess of your life, if there are areas that need to be cleaned up, it's time to go back and pick up after yourself—in other words, take responsibility for your actions. In the movie *Courageous*, one of the characters got a young lady pregnant and abandoned her to raise their child by herself. After years of being an absentee dad, he realized how selfish he had been.

He ended up writing her a letter, including some money and explaining that he wanted to take steps to start making things right. Perhaps one of the most beautiful scenes in the movie is when he sees his daughter for the first time. He realized he had made a mess and was willing to go back and make things right.[12] You might not be an absentee dad who abandoned your child, but are there areas in your life that you need to clean up?

Are there relationships that need to be restored? Is there someone you've hurt with harsh words and won't talk to? Is there someone you feel like you disappointed and now you're avoiding them? Whatever your situation, do your part to make things right. Aim to always leave things better off than when you first found them. Learn to say sorry, but not only that, to show you are by your actions.

REFLECTION EXERCISE

1. When in a situation where you should apologize, how likely are you to do so:

   Very Likely   Likely   Somewhat Likely   Not Likely

   Very Unlikely

2. Can you think of anyone who you owe an apology to? List them.

3. What is keeping you back from apologizing to the other person? Is it worth it? Write your answer.

42

WHEN YOU TRY TO BE A
BLESSING AND IT BACKFIRES

When you try to be a blessing to someone it could backfire. If you haven't already experienced this, brace yourself for the impact of the pain that comes with helping someone who ends up hurting you. Just don't let that stop you from ever wanting to be a blessing again.

A few years ago, I met a man who had invited his nieces and nephews to Thanksgiving dinner. He spent hours shopping, prepping, and cooking this great meal by himself. The night before Thanksgiving he called each one to make sure they were still coming. They all confirmed they would be there. He woke up early that morning, finished all the last-minute cooking he needed to do, set the table, and got everything prepared.

A couple of hours went by—and still—nobody showed up. He finally called one of his nieces to find out if she was on the way. Sadly, she, along with all the other family members said they weren't going to make it. This man told me he would never do Thanksgiving dinner for his family again. I understand why he might have felt that way, but the problem wasn't with his generosity.

The problem was with the recipients of his generosity. If you've tried to be a blessing and it didn't work out, don't give up on it.

43

LET GOD FIGHT YOUR BATTLES

The best fights are the ones that never happen! You're probably not the type of guy that would back down from a fight. If somebody wants to start something you're ready to go toe-to-toe. I understand that mindset. I regularly train in Krav Maga, a self-defense system that is swift and can even be lethal.

One of the things we're taught is to move forward and close in on our opponent. But we're also taught that there are times where you need to disengage—to get out of dodge. I learned early on, as a young Marine, drooling at the tongue for a fight, that the best fights to win are the ones that you place in God's hands and watch him work His *magic*.

It was during combat training and we were tasked with night watch. The Marine in charge of making the schedule placed me on it five days in a row. The issue with this was that we had enough Marines to cover the entire period we were in training, and no one was supposed to have night watch more than once.

When I approached him about it, he threw his clipboard down, got in my face, and told me to "mind my own business" because he was the one in charge of making the schedule and could do whatever he wanted. Back then it didn't take much for me to reach the point of spontaneous combustion. I was like a grenade with the pin pulled that was just seconds away from exploding. Surprisingly, that's not what happened.

Before I said a word I paused, looked up at the sky, and said, "God, you got this," then I walked away. When I woke up the next morning, I peeked my head out of my tent to see who was making that high-pitched screeching sound. Guess who it was? It was my little *friend* who was "in charge." He was being attacked by a swarm of bees. From that point on, I was never scheduled for watch again.

This was a fight I was glad I let God handle for me. My way of handling it wouldn't have been as effective. Sometimes you'll face things that seem like an uphill battle. Maybe there's somebody you wish would change, a boss or coworker who's the reason behind why you dread going to work.

Whatever it is, are you willing to step aside and see God fight your battles? Sometimes it means not saying a word. Sometimes it means letting someone make decisions for themselves instead of trying to "make them" do what you want. Have you been fighting a battle that's time for you to back down from and turn over to God?

44

DON'T HATE, COLLABORATE

What guy doesn't like a little bit of competition? It's healthy. That's part of what drives us to be our best. I thrive most when I'm surrounded by people who are at a higher level than I am. It pushes me to want to do better. When you're around people who are moving in the direction you want to go in, or who are already there, you can either be a "hater", or you can be a "collaborator."

When you see someone who's successful, it probably took a lot for him to get where he is. As my brother says, "You don't know the story behind the glory." In other words, all you can see is the final product, but you don't know the struggles he had to go through to get there.

What I've noticed that's hard for a lot of guys to do is congratulate each other for their successes. This happens when you have a hard time dealing with the fact that someone has something you don't. It's called insecurity. Whenever that happens, the only way you can truly be happy for them is to humble yourself and understand that just because someone has what you're working toward or what you don't have, it doesn't make you any less of a man.

It makes you a bigger man when you can learn to not be a "hater," but be a "congratulator, and take it a step further and even become a "collaborator." You'll have much more victory and impact in your life when you learn how to ask the next man what his key to success is.

When you see someone who's trying to get to where you are, you can either be intimidated by their drive and motivation to succeed, or you can offer to help them. If you're on the job and someone wants to know something, will you keep your knowledge to yourself for fear that they might take your position or outdo you? Or will you decide to collaborate with them to help them achieve success? Don't "hate," collaborate.

45

DON'T MAKE BAD DECISIONS TO PLEASE GOOD PEOPLE

Don't make bad decisions to please good people; this is what happens to people-pleasers. My wife and I had been married almost a year and had no children. I was about to leave to go to combat and there were people in my family who told me I needed to make sure my wife was pregnant before I left. They wanted to make sure I had a child in case something happened, and I died while I was deployed.

These were good people who genuinely loved me, but I couldn't allow myself to make a decision I knew my wife and I weren't ready for just to please them. Sometimes doing what you know is right might not make others happy, but it just takes courage to do the right thing anyway. If you're a people pleaser, you're going to struggle with making decisions like this. If you're reading this and thinking to yourself, "this section is not for me at all," that's probably because you could care less what others think.

That can be a strong quality to have because you will be a man of conviction, but it's also good to be careful not to quickly dismiss others you trust who have good advice to share with you. It's okay to get input from others. Just make sure the decisions you make are not the result of feeling guilty or the need to be a people-pleaser. Don't make bad decisions to please good people.

REFLECTION EXERCISE

1. Have you ever made a decision you regretted because you were trying to be a people-pleaser? If so, describe it:

2. If so, how did it make you feel? Did it motivate you to do better or did it create feelings of insecurity and jealousy?

3. What things do you consider when trying to make decisions? (Your dreams and goals, how it affects others, principles, potential outcomes, what type of person you are or strive to be, etc.).

46

SCRATCH MY BACK AND GIVE ME A PILLOW

It's amazing how the smallest gesture can make send the message that you care. If you're a dad, husband, big brother, or leader of any kind, I'm sure you want to have a positive influence in the lives of those around you. Sometimes it comes by doing the little things.

One day as my family sat on the couch enjoying a movie night, I noticed one of my daughters was trying miserably to scratch her back. I reached my hand over and scratched her back. A few seconds later, she was struggling to position her pillow behind her neck. I reach over and fixed it for her.

The smile that came across her face was like a billboard advertisement that said, "Life is good; I've got it made!' What I did probably meant nothing to anyway else, but to my daughter, it meant the world. There are things you can do for others that would make a world of difference. If you're a leader who's used to other people doing tasks for you, try doing something for them that makes them feel like you met a need they had.

On another note, if you're under a leader who has a lot on his plate, try seeing what you can do to make life a little better for him or her and see where it takes you. You reap what you sow; show that you're willing to serve and help them accomplish their mission. People take notice of the little things you do and will remember them. Don't let your status prevent you from serving others.

47

MAKE IT A POINT TO SAY THANK YOU

You send a powerful message when you say thank you. Just this simple act of kindness, which doesn't cost you anything, can make a big impact on someone's day. One day I was at Subway getting my usual tuna melt. I noticed that the gentleman behind the counter washed his hands before putting on a new pair of gloves (this was before COVID-19). I complimented him for taking the time to wash his hands.

He shook his head, smiled, and looked down at the counter before telling me about his previous customer. "Thanks for saying that. About forty minutes ago a lady nearly yelled at me because she said I didn't wash my hands good enough." One simple compliment took him from feeling bad to being encouraged.

I've chosen to be different. If you've worked in any type of job that requires customer service, you know that some of the people you deal with are ungrateful and rude. You can choose to be different and make a positive impact in the world instead of bringing negativity. There's enough of that on the news.

When I'm out shopping, if I see somebody that's doing a great job, who has a good attitude, and is trying to represent their company well, I'll usually ask them to speak to their manager.

Each time I make this request, they look like someone who just got pulled over for speeding and is about to get a ticket.

After this, a manager usually comes up looking like someone who's prepared for a fistfight. After my usual smile and a short "Hi, I wanted to recognize one of your employees because I thought they did a phenomenal job," the manager stands there for a couple of seconds with nothing to say before snapping back into reality.

They were expecting yet another angry, disgruntled customer who had a list of complaints, but instead, they got somebody who was there to compliment them on a job well done. This makes the manager's day too. Make it a point to be different, to not take out your frustrations on the person behind the counter who's got a kid at home and is probably tired and struggling to get by. Go out of your way to say thank you and show your appreciation. It makes a difference.

Part Four

PREPARE FOR IMPACT

48

PREPARE FOR IMPACT

Whenever a flight crew expects to make a crash landing, everyone aboard is instructed to "prepare/brace for impact." Imagine sitting on a flight and suddenly feeling like you hit a big speed bump in the sky. Shortly after that, the plane feels like the engine has been turned off and you begin dropping altitude quickly.

At that moment, you're praying to God that you can make it through this. You're also hoping the pilots are prepared to handle this type of situation. You're depending on them. This is what life is like for a lot of people around you. You're all on the same plane. They hit speed bumps and are hoping someone can come along and help guide them toward safety.

Yet sometimes you feel like an untrained pilot who barely knows how to fly through your own problems, let alone help someone else through theirs. I want to encourage you to believe that you do have something to offer the world. You can make a far greater impact than you could ever realize.

You never know where God will take you, or who He will want you to make an impact on. You might end up helping somebody fly through danger and defeat so they can land toward safety and victory. You don't know when your chance will come but stay prepared and be on the lookout. If you don't like the idea of flying, you're going to have to come up with another analogy on your own—sorry. The point is, there are all kinds of opportunities for you to make an impact. Don't stay stuck where you are because you're afraid to fly. People are depending on you.

49

DON'T UNDERESTIMATE
THE POWER OF YOUR GIFT

Somebody needs what you have. Don't underestimate the power of your gift. Find what you're passionate about and look for healthy ways to enjoy and share it with the world. One of my favorite things to do is to play music and sing. It's one of the things I'm passionate about. I remember growing up in Motown. My dad would take me downtown to Hart Plaza to play jazz music.

While I played, he had people pass by and drop money into my instrument case. Although we didn't spend as much time as I would have liked to, music was one of the ways my dad and I bonded. It's been a big part of my life. I've chosen to use my musical gifts in a way that can positively impact people.

My wife and I recently started a YouTube channel called "Music and Marriage." This is one of the ways we use our passion to make an impact. We provide inspirational music as well as candid conversations about marriage to help encourage other couples. Nothing is too small to be used to make an impact on others.

Let's say you have a passion for comic books. You might not think that's something that you can use to make a difference in the world. But what if you used your passion for comics to teach lessons about life to kids in your community? Teach them about having good values and using their strength to help others rather than for selfish reasons. Use your gifts to make the world a better place.

50

YOU DON'T HAVE TO BE A MILLIONAIRE
TO MAKE A DIFFERENCE

You don't have to be a millionaire to make a difference. I had an aunt who would save up a small amount of her paycheck throughout the year. Then just before winter, she would find kids in the neighborhood whose parents were struggling. She made sure as many children as possible had jackets for the winter. She found a way to make a difference in her community. She never allowed the fact that she was on a low income to prevent her from making a difference.

If you're paying attention, you will have countless opportunities to make a difference. I never thought a stranger would have wanted to hug me, especially during the first few months of COVID-19. That's exactly what happened and there was nothing I could do about it. I stood in line behind an elderly couple while the clerk rang up their groceries. The woman swiped her card several times but each time the machine made that infamous beep letting us know the transaction didn't process.

She turned toward her husband, hid her face in her hands, and then looked up as though she was pleading with God to help her. I asked the clerk if I could pay for her groceries, and before I left, the old lady I helped lunged forward and nearly tackled me with her bearhug. I can only imagine what it would have been like for this elderly couple who spent all that time shopping, ringing up everything, only to leave the store empty-handed.

Times are tough right now for a lot of people. If doing something like this is within your reach, you can be an example of something positive happening in the world. You don't have to be rich to make a difference. Use what you have, where you are, and make a positive impact.

51

GIVING BACK

One of the greatest ways you can make an impact is by volunteering in your community. Besides that, there are some benefits you enjoy when you give your time and money for a good cause. A few years ago, I began volunteering with Habitat for Humanity. One day while working I was offered a job on the spot by one of the contractors.

They liked the work I did and thought they could use someone like me on their team. I was excited that they would even consider me, especially considering my experience level was next to nothing. I didn't end up taking the offer, but that's just an example of what happens when you're trying to give back.

Plus, I got a chance to meet some great people and work with my hands doing things I wouldn't normally do. It felt good knowing that I was helping build a house somebody would one day enjoy. An article put out by Western Connecticut State University gives some of the other benefits of volunteering:[13]

-Brings fun and fulfillment to your life

-You can learn valuable job skills

-You can try out a new career before you jump all in

-Can help increase your happiness

-Can help you stay healthy

-Can help you combat depression

There are a lot of options out there, but to help you get started, here are a few ways you can volunteer in your community.

Opportunities to Make an Impact by Volunteering

■   Volunteer for CASA (Court Appointed Special Advocate) https://nationalcasagal.org/our-work/mission-vision-and-values/

"The National CASA/GAL Association, together with state and local member programs, supports and promotes court-appointed volunteer advocacy so every child who has experienced abuse or neglect can be safe, have a permanent home, and the opportunity to thrive."

■   Volunteer for Habitat for Humanity https://www.habitat.org/volunteer

This is a great way for you to support a good cause, meet new people, and learn or use those handyman skills.

■   Volunteer for *SCORE* (Senior Core of Retired Executives) https://www.score.org/volunteer

This is a great way to establish some good relationships and surround yourself with entrepreneurs. Here are some of the ways you can volunteer:

-Become a mentor who helps others with their business startups

-Teach Workshops and Classes

-Serve in a support role

- *Volunteer Match*
  https://www.volunteermatch.org/

This is a great way to find volunteer opportunities in your area. You might be surprised to find opportunities that range from volunteering at a professional sporting event to helping at a local food bank.

- *Crisis Textline*
  https://www.crisistextline.org/become-a-volunteer/

Receive free training valued at over $1,000 to become a volunteer crisis counselor. In exchange, you commit to volunteering to be on standby for four hours a week until you reach a total of 200 hours.

- Red Cross

- Toys for Tots Program

- Serving in a Local Church

52

LEAD FROM THE FRONT

I magine showing up to work one day and having your boss tell you that in three months everyone is required to run a half-marathon (13.1 miles). And oh, by the way, you're going to run at least three times each week, one of them being a 10-miler. Unless you just love running, you probably would be ready to put in your two-week notice. I ran cross country and track in high school, yet even I hated the idea of doing something like this.

I still run today—not ten miles—but I can still hear my commanding officer's voice: "Lead from the front!" If you were in a position of leadership, you had men who were expecting you to give 110%. That meant you needed to be and do what you expected of them. In other words, lead by example. Whether you realize it or not, someone is always watching you.

Don't expect from others, what they don't see from you. One of the things I heard growing up was, "Son, I'm doing this, but you don't do it!" Those were words that came from my dad, a man who loved me with all his heart yet struggled to be the example he wanted me to one day live out.

I'm deeply grateful for the many life lessons he taught me, but I wonder how much more powerful they might have been if paired with his example. It's a struggle to do sometimes but don't forget that you need to lead from the front and set a good example with what you say and do.

REFLECTION EXERCISE

1. Is there anybody in your life who looks up to you and will follow the example you set?

2. Do you struggle to lead from the front? If so, write down some areas you can do better at?

3. What would you have to do differently to start "leading from the front the way you should?"

Part Five

MONEY HABITS

53

THE $200 RULE

I know what it's like to struggle and be stressed out trying to deal with the result of not making wise decisions with my money. There's a lot to talk about when it comes to finances, but I just want to briefly talk about a few important topics. Before I started this book, I was writing a book on finances.

I'd already finished the first draft, hired a professional editor, and spent hours making revisions. In the future, I'll be releasing a book on finances that goes more in-depth. For right now, I just want to give you some tips to help you experience victory in your finances.

While in the Marines I once had a roommate who bought a brand-new Ford Mustang. He spent all $400 of his first paycheck on the car payment. He spent his other paycheck for the month on his car insurance, which was also $400. Since he lived in military housing, he didn't have to pay rent and all his meals were taken care of, so at least he had food and a place to stay.

It was sad to walk by his Mustang on the way to work in the mornings, knowing all it was going to do was just sit there. He couldn't even afford to put gas in his car. This was a bad decision he struggled with for a while. I've had my share of problems with

151

high car payments, so I know what it feels like. Maybe one day we'll be able to afford to pay cash for a nearly new car without having to worry about car payments. Until then, one of the most responsible things I feel I can do is to make sure that we don't overextend ourselves by getting a car payment that we can't keep up with.

When I walk into a car dealership, I know that one of the first things they're going to ask me is how much money I want to pay each month. I never have to worry about that because I come with a pre-approved check and usually have already done my homework, so I know exactly which type of car I'm going to buy and how much I'd like to spend on it.

My goal is to have a car payment that hovers right around $200.00. I've bought three nice, reliable cars using this method. Ultimately, not having a car payment is the goal, but after negotiating the price—putting money down, and doing the numbers I want to make sure that if I had no income coming in, I could still somehow afford my car.

Two hundred dollars is such a low amount that I could probably make that amount doing deliveries for a few days out of the week if I ever had to. To make sure I stay within my $200 rule, I either have to put *more* money down or get a lower-priced car. I don't believe in high car payments, and I also don't believe in paying the full asking price from the dealer.

When you buy a brand-new car unless you do some negotiating—which I highly recommend—you're paying full price. You're stuck eating the depreciation on it. You might have heard someone say that as soon as you drive the car off the lot it loses its value. "Most new cars depreciate [drop in value] 40%-50% during the first three years of ownership."[14]

My suggestion: *never* pay full price for a new car. Either get a new car that was released in the last couple of years or get a used one that's in great condition. Ramit Sethi gives some excellent ideas to help you decide between purchasing a new or used car. He also talks about some ways you can save money regardless of which one you buy.[15]

If you decide to go the used car route, it might be helpful to have a mechanic inspect the car before purchasing it. The last thing you want is to run in and out of the repair shop every month. The $200 rule has worked well for me over the years, but no matter what amount you choose, the principle remains the same: don't get more car than you can afford.

54

MY CRAZY WAY OF SAVING

My philosophy on saving is much different than probably any financial expert I've ever listened to. I remember when I was so broke, I couldn't even afford gas money to get back home after work. At least I had a car—but still—my financial life was a mess.

I even had to ask a coworker for some money who had a wife and several children—yet I was single with no other responsibilities. I look back on those days now and all I can do is shake my head. I eventually reached a point where I had to make some big changes.

I had so much debt I didn't even know where to start. All I knew was I needed to pay off all my credit cards and take care of anything that was in collections. For some reason, I had the silly idea to start putting $500 away in savings every month. I don't know what I was thinking.

Who in the world saves $500 when they're in as much debt as I was? That's exactly what I did. The crazy thing is that God somehow still allowed me to be able to gain ground tackling my debt. From that point on, anytime I got extra money, I would use it to pay off debt.

Since I was already in debt anyway, I decided I might as well have some type of savings to fall back on if I needed it. I just want to make sure you know that I'm *not* suggesting that you go out today and open a savings account and start throwing hundreds of dollars into it. That's not what I'm saying at all.

I *am* suggesting, however, that even if you put away 5 dollars each paycheck, at least you'll get in the habit of having something saved up. You can build from there, but you *have to* start somewhere. How you handle your money can either be a source of heartache or it can be a source of blessing.

Eventually, you want to work your way up to where you can save at least 20% of your income. If you're not comfortable with my method, maybe you could try saving a portion of your next pay raise. Whether you decide to try my crazy way of saving or not, it's always helpful for you to seek out advice from a professional who can help you get your finances straight. The key is that you get started.

55

HAVE A SPENDING PLAN

I don't know where all my money is going. Is that a familiar phrase? That's because your money won't do what you don't tell it to. If you don't keep track of what you make and spend and have some type of written plan, it's never too late to start. You can have a better financial situation, but you have to be willing to do what it takes to get there. It's a lot easier to spend than it is to keep track of *what* you spend.

Have you ever heard the saying, "Time flies, but you're the pilot?" The same holds true for money. It seems to fly away on its own—and it will unless you take control. One of the best ways to do this is by having a spending plan. If you haven't already completed the exercises in the section titled, "I Want More Out of Life," where you wrote out your goals and dreams, please complete that before doing the exercise in this chapter.

Your spending plan should have the following five characteristics:

1. It Reflects your goals: for example if your goal is to purchase a new home, but you're spending hundreds of dollars on clothes and eating out each month, how can you expect to get where you want to be?

2. It's worthy of commitment: If looking at your spending plan gives you the thought of wanting to ball it up and throw it away, it's not something you're going to stick with. You have to be honest with yourself and the level of commitment you're willing to make. So, if you know you're only willing to save fifty dollars when you know you should be saving one hundred, it's better to consistently save the lower amount, than it is to set the higher goal, constantly fail, and then eventually stop saving altogether.

3. It's not stuck in your head: A plan that stays in your head is less likely to become a reality. It can be as simple as grabbing a sheet of paper and writing out all the money you earn, expenses you have, and savings goals. You can get an app or use an excel spreadsheet. The main thing is that it's written and in a format you feel comfortable with.

4. Leaves room for ice cream: If your plan leaves no room for fun, it's going to be very hard to stick to. Even if all you do is get your favorite snack once a week, do it.

5. Leaves room for spills: Things we can't control will always happen. Somewhere in your spending plan, you should leave room for things like a flat tire or car repair.

"Making and sticking to a budget is a key step towards getting a handle on your debt and working towards a savings goal, of any kind."[16] Part of financial victory is having and following a plan. Following is an exercise that can help you get a jumpstart toward putting together a budget and sticking to it.

SPENDING PLAN EXERCISE

Instructions: Go to the Consumer Financial Protection Bureau website and pull up the article titled: "Budgeting: How to create a budget and stick with it." Use the article to answer the questions that follow. Download any additional templates or trackers you see on their website. There are a ton of other resources, but this is just one. You'll go through the following steps to complete this exercise:

Step 1: Identify and record where your money comes from

Step 2: Identify and record where your money has been going

Step 3: Identify and record all your expenses and bills, along with their due dates

Step 4: Create your working budget

Additional things to consider:

-Automating as many bills and expenses as you can

-If necessary, getting someone who can hold you accountable and help you stay on track

-Plugging your numbers into an app after completing this exercise to make things simpler

56

DOES MONEY MAKE YOU HAPPY?

Materialism is the breeding ground for success without joy! As a child, I remember running to the mailbox to check for new sales papers (aka junk mail): the ones you don't want, hardly read, and wonder why they send them in the first place.

I would flip to the toy section and daydream about which new remote-control car I wanted to add to my Christmas wish list. I even cut out pictures of my favorite toys. At seven years old this type of thinking was probably harmless, but for an adult to place this high of a value on material possessions, it's a recipe for unhappiness. Scott Dawson and Marsha Richins are scientists who spent two decades studying the relationship between materialism and how it affects a person's happiness.

They found that the people who scored high in materialism usually showed a lower score on tests used to measure happiness.[17] The Merriam-Webster Dictionary defines materialism in two ways. "A doctrine that the only or the highest value or objectives lie in material progress," and "a preoccupation with or stress upon material rather than intellectual or spiritual things."[18]

As a child, I got to see a real-life example of materialism. My uncle took me along to his dad's birthday party. While there his dad hardly talked about anything else except the expensive new camera he had just bought. My uncle looked at me and said, "Dak, you see how he's so caught up in showing everyone his camera? That's not what's important. The things that are important in life are family and friends."

What a great lesson to learn as a little boy. That's the exact opposite of what the commercial industry pushes. What do you see when you drive down the road? What about when you turn on the TV or browse through a website? Chances are, you'll see some type of advertisement. What's the big deal with advertisements? Isn't that how businesses attract new customers?

Companies don't just make products so they can sit there and pat themselves on the back and tell each other how great they are. They're trying to convince you why you can't live without it. When you feel that tug toward materialism, remember this quote by Devin Thorpe: "In the end, it will not matter how much money you had or what you accomplished. What will matter are your family and the legacy you leave behind: the mark you leave on the world."

57

STAY ON TOP OF YOUR CREDIT

Not taking care of your credit can cause a lot of stress and anxiety. It's important to maintain good credit. Having bad credit could also prevent you from being able to move your family into a nice home, cost you a lot of extra money in interest payments, or prevent you from getting hired for certain job positions. I put together a free 5-Day mini-course to help you learn what you need to do to work on improving your credit. Here are the topics I cover:

Day 1 Goal: You Will Pull Your Credit Report

1. Where to Get Your Credit Report

2. The Process of Pulling Your Credit Report

3. How Often to Check Your Credit Report

Day 2 Goal: Review Your Credit Report for Questionable or Inaccurate Info

1. Reviewing Your Credit Report for Accuracy

2. Identifying Negative Trends on Your Credit Report

Day 3 Goal: Download and Review Template for Preparing a Dispute Letter

1. How to Submit Disputes to Correct Errors

2. Using the "Whole Truth Statement" to explain negative
     information on your credit report

Day 4 Goal: Fill out Dispute Letter/Whole Truth Statement or Get Caught Up on Previous Days

Day 5 Goal: Place a Freeze on Your Credit Report; Opt-out of Pre-Approved Credit Offers

1. Protecting Yourself from Credit Fraud

2. Best Practices for Maintaining Good Credit and Tackling Debt

Sign-up for this Free Mini-Course at:
https://habitsforgrowth.com/goodcredit/

58

WHAT'S ALL THE HYPE ABOUT
STARTING A BUSINESS?

I t's easier than ever to start a business today. If you have access to the Internet, you can do something that will generate you more money. Opportunities to generate income are even available in the gig economy. If you have a car you're not using, you might be able to make money by leaving it at the airport over the weekend and allowing people to rent it out. You can rent out storage space.

If you're breathing, you can have a business that makes you some type of money. The options are endless. If you're trying to make some extra money but you're not interested in starting your own business, visit www.gigeconomyjobslist.com/ for a long list of side gigs you can do.

I won't speak much about being an entrepreneur until I gain success in this area myself—maybe in a future book I'll be able to. For now, here is a list of resources I use to learn more about building a business that makes an impact. Please take advantage of these resources so you can get in on what I see so many people moving toward being an entrepreneur.

RESOURCES FOR STARTING A BUSINESS

-*SCORE* (Senior Core of Retired Executives) "offers free live and recorded webinars & interactive courses-on-demand on small business topics ranging from startup strategies to marketing and financing."

Take free workshops: https://www.score.org/take-workshop

Get free one-on-one mentorship at any stage of your business: https://www.score.org/find-mentor

-*SBA (U.S. Small Business Administration)*

This site has a ton of resources to help you plan, launch, manage, and grow a business.
https://www.sba.gov/business-guide

-*Fiverr*

This is a great resource for any new entrepreneur who doesn't have a big budget. You can easily find people to make logos, build websites, marketing research, etc.
www.fiverr.com/

Write a Book (your life story, expertise, fiction, etc.)

-*Self-Publishing Books 101:*
A Step-by-Step Guide to Publishing Your Book in Multiple Formats by Shelley Hitz and Heather Hart. This book is available on Amazon Kindle for free and is packed with a ton of useful tips to help you.

-Bookbound Online Workshop by Michelle Prince

This is a great resource that will take you through the entire process of what it takes to write and publish a book. You take the course online at your own pace and can revisit it as many times as you want.

www.bookboundonline.com

Christian Book Academy

This is an excellent resource if you want to write a book but don't know where to start. One of their goals is "to take you from being stuck in fear and overwhelm to publishing the book you were created to write with peace and clarity."

www.christianbookacademy.com

-Kingdom Writers: A Podcast for Christian Writers of All Genres

This is one of the best podcasts for learning how to write a book, learn creative ways to market, and get inspirational tips to encourage you.

www.trainingauthors.com/subscribe/

Podcasts for Business and Marketing

-Smart Passive Income by Pat Flynn

-Online Marketing Made Easy by Amy Porterfield

-Podcastification by Carey Greene

-The Blogging Millionaire by Brandon Gaille

-Lead to Win: Michael Hyatt and Megan Hyatt Miller

Part Six

DEALING WITH DARK MOMENTS

59

I JUST WANT TO BE BY MYSELF

When you start feeling like you just want to be by yourself, you're in the beginning stages of a slow, painful numbing of your senses to everything helpful and good for you. When things start getting rough do you stop reaching out to your family and friends? Do you stop answering phone calls and messages?

A lot of people who find themselves in this situation don't want to be a burden to the people they care about. So what do they end up doing? They try to shield themselves from anyone finding out they hit a rough spot spiritually, mentally, or emotionally. A lot of men do this: drawing away from people is their first reaction when things go wrong. When you do this, you could be headed down a dangerous path.

If even the most hardened criminals are crushed by being in isolation, what do you think it will do to you over time? I understand that with the COVID-19 pandemic, many of us have experienced isolation in some form. But when you go into isolation, you sometimes remove yourself from the reach of others helping you. I've been there and it's not a fun place.

Don't ever think your situation is so bad that you can't get help. And don't waste away in silence, allowing yourself to remain defeated because you're afraid of being a burden on someone. In the next chapter, I'm going to include some resources for you to get help if you need it.

60

WHEN DARK MOMENTS COME

Statistics show that "suicide is the 10th leading cause of death in the U.S."[19] I realize this is a book on how to live a life of victory. So why talk about suicide? It's a sad reality, but even the toughest men have responded to dark moments by taking their own lives.

If life were full of roses and we never had any problems, there would be no need for me writing this book, but the reality is that at some point in life, you're bound to have dark moments. A loved one will pass away, tragedy may strike unexpectedly, a major disappointment could occur. Growing up I had a very happy childhood, and when I became an adult, I couldn't understand how someone could even *think* of taking their own lives.

Then it happened. There I was, twenty-one years old, a Sergeant in the Marines, yet I felt hopeless. There were many days I thought about just driving my car straight into oncoming traffic. I'm glad I never attempted anything but unfortunately, I know people who can't say the same. I wrote this section because I know suicide is a very real issue many people deal with.

That's why it's important to have some type of idea or plan for dealing with dark moments, should they come. When a thunderstorm comes and knocks out the power in your neighborhood, if you don't know where your flashlight is, it's a little too late to go and buy one. You should already have one just in case you ever need it. Many of the men who end up in low places have no plan in place to be able to find their *flashlight*, to help them navigate their way out of their dark moments.

I'm begging you to please consider having a mental health/crisis plan regardless of how tough you think you are. I've included a list of resources here that will help you know where to start if you're experiencing dark moments. Sometimes you need to learn healthy ways to cope with the challenges you're facing. If you honestly want help, I believe that as you start looking into the resources listed here, you'll begin to find even more tools that will help you.

If you're dealing with these types of thoughts, I know what it's like. I've been there. If you deal with depression or suicidal thoughts, there's hope. If I could personally help you, I would, but I'm not a counselor and all I can do is try to point you in the right direction. Following are mental health, substance abuse, and suicide prevention resources to at least give you a starting point.

Please, get the help you need before it's too late. If this isn't something you deal with, save these resources so you can help someone else who might need it.

-National Suicide Prevention Lifeline: 800-273-8255
To chat online: https://suicidepreventionlifeline.org/chat/
https://suicidepreventionlifeline.org/

-The Veterans Crisis Line: 800-273-8255 and press 1 (24/7)
Text 838255 (24/7)
Online chat: http://www.veteranscrisisline.net/get-help/chat

-SAMHSA's National Helpline (Substance Abuse):
800-662-4357
This organization does not provide counseling. SAMHSA has trained information specialists who answer calls, transfer callers to state services or other appropriate intake centers in their states, and connect them with local assistance and support. If you or someone you know is struggling with an addiction, this can help jumpstart you toward the road of recovery.
https://www.samhsa.gov/find-help/national-helpline

-FaithfulCounseling
Faithful Counseling is designed as a solution for people seeking traditional mental health counseling who would prefer hearing from the perspective of a Christian. You do not have to be a Christian to use this service. If you have financial constraints, they have a financial assistance program you can apply for to help you pay for your counseling.
https://www.faithfulcounseling.com/

-Mental Health First Aid Training
This is a free one-day course where you'll learn how to help someone who may be experiencing a mental health or substance abuse challenge. Just like you would do a course on CPR in case you need to help someone, this course is similar. Taking this course might even help you map out your own mental health/crisis plan. Learn more about it and find a location near you that offers the course:
https://www.mentalhealthfirstaid.org/take-a-course/what-you-learn/

-How to Support a Family Member or Friend Who's Battling Depression

This article discusses warning signs of depression, ways to encourage others to seek help, and how to be alert to the warning signs of suicide. If you battle with depression or know someone who does, read this article:

https://www.mayoclinic.org/diseases-conditions/depression/in-depth/depression/art-20045943

-DIY (Do-it-yourself) Workbooks to Build Stronger Mental Health

These extremely helpful workbooks were put together by the Positive Psychology Research Group. These are **free workbooks** that would cost hundreds of dollars if you had to pay for them, but you can click any of the following books to download them at no cost. This isn't a direct download link, but if you go to the following website, just look for DIY Workbooks and you'll find books on several topics:

evworthington-forgiveness.com/

61

HELP! I'M STRUGGLING TO FIND MY PURPOSE

The greatest life you'll ever live is one that flows from knowing God and fulfilling the purpose He created you for. I know guys who will run up and down a basketball court for hours without complaining. If I took those same group of guys outside and told them to run for thirty minutes, what would happen?

They probably wouldn't do too well. That's because when you remove the basketball and rim, you remove their purpose for running. They no longer have the drive or motivation they need. Living your life without purpose is not much different. You're just running from place to place, dragging yourself out of bed in the morning, and sometimes doubting whether it's even worth it.

I don't know if anyone ever told you this, but if not, you need to know. You'll never truly be satisfied without knowing God and fulfilling the purpose he created you for. Some men go from relationship to relationship hoping to find happiness. Others pursue dreams and careers in hopes of getting to the top. After a while, they begin to ask themselves, "Is there more to life than this?" Even after reaching their goals and achieving great success, they're still left with a deep sense that something is missing. This is a story

I can relate to. By the time I was twenty-one, I'd already bought my first home, a luxury car, and advanced to levels of promotion as a Marine that placed me years ahead of my peers. Despite all of this, I still had this sense that something was missing. You can have all these things like I did, yet still not feel like you truly know what your purpose is. That was my story.

Eventually, I discovered the problem. I was the *boss* of my own life. I was the one that called all the *shots*. It's not like I completely shut God out, but I lived for whatever made me happy and sometimes didn't care about the consequences. I was trying to make life work on my own terms, which left me nowhere. Since I held this supreme position in my life, I was unwilling to give control over to God.

I eventually realized some things about God that made me want to give my life over to Him. I wasn't just looking for Him to give me a break financially or make my life better. I reached a point where I felt like I needed Him. I wanted to know more about Him. I'm glad somebody took the time to share with me how I could know Him personally—not just as my Creator who provides for me, but as my Savior who died for me.

Let me introduce you to Him. One thing I'm promised is that no matter how bad things get down here on earth, I have something better to look forward to in Heaven. What I'm about to tell you helped me answer questions I had like, "Why am I even alive?" "What's my purpose in life?" Here's what I learned that completely changed my life.

1. I realized that I offended God by breaking His law and was not in a right relationship with Him (I was unrighteous). In fact, I was an enemy of God. (Romans. 3:10; 3:23; James 4:4).

2. He knew I couldn't go to church, pray, or do enough good things to work my way into being in good standing with Him. In God's eyes, my attempts to make myself clean from sin were no different than trying to use a muddy cloth to remove a stain from a shirt. I needed something outside of my own efforts. (Isaiah 64:6; Romans 5:6; Ephesians 2:8-9).

3. I realized that even though God is a Judge, He doesn't want anyone to receive the ultimate sentence of being eternally separated from Him (Romans 6:23; Revelation 20:14-15). His will is for everyone to be saved (2 Peter 3:9). God made a way to still judge my sin yet make it to where I wasn't the one who had to suffer the consequence of paying for them. To do that, He sent Jesus to die on the cross in my place to be my substitute (John 3:16; Romans 5:8; 2 Corinthians 5:21).

4. God didn't force me to receive this gift. I made a choice to surrender control of my life and the sins I loved, so I could follow God. I made a decision to trust that what Jesus did by dying on the cross was enough to pay for and erase all my sins. (Romans 10:9-10). If you don't already know what it's like to have a personal relationship with Christ, I truly hope that one day you will. Don't put it off though because tomorrow isn't promised (Luke 12:16-21; James 4:14).

62

WHEN YOU MAKE A MESS OF YOUR LIFE

Is it possible for you to be so messed up and in such a dark place that even God doesn't want to have anything to do with you? You've messed up so bad you believe there's no way God could ever forgive you. I've experienced that as well. One morning while brushing my teeth I looked up at the mirror as tears began to stream down my face. I could barely get the words out, but I prayed aloud: "God, do you still love me?"

One of the saddest things I've ever heard someone say was, "Why am I even still alive?" I never said that, but I reached such a low point in my life I didn't even know if God loved me anymore. It seemed like everything was messed up in my life. I was broke, in debt, depressed, and even suicidal at times. I was partying my life away, wasting time, and felt like my life had no purpose.

I had a lot of outward success, but on the inside, I was empty. Two strange things happened the same day I prayed and asked God if He still loved me. When I got to work my boss called me into his office, which is something that rarely happened first thing in the morning. I felt like I was waiting on the results from a serious medical test or something. I had no idea what he was going to say.

To my surprise, his first words were, "Do you have a pen?" I slowly reached for my pen as the look on my face changed.

"What is this all about? He pulls me into his office to ask me for a pen?" What he told me next left me with my hand under my chin and the biggest smile I'd had in months. "I got a call from headquarters, and they said you have a $16,500 bonus."

After I left his office, I looked up, smiled, and whispered a prayer: "I guess you do still love me, God." As I continued my day all I could think about was my prayer in front of the mirror and the conversation with my boss. That same day while waiting at the car wash, an old lady walked up to me, placed her hand on my shoulder, and said she didn't know why, but the Lord was directing her to pray for me.

Right there in the middle of the car wash, that lady prayed the most powerful prayer I'd ever heard in my life. I knew this was God's way of showing me just how much he loved me. No matter where you are in life or how bad it gets, never forget: God still loves you!

Part Seven

HEALTHY HABITS

63

DO YOUR OWN RESEARCH

Take care of your health today, in a way you won't regret tomorrow. SM Lockridge, a great preacher of the past once talked about how people waste their health trying to get wealth then spend their wealth trying to regain the health they wasted. In this section, I will give you a few tips on things you can do to stay healthy.

I can't stress enough how important it is for you to become more informed when it comes to taking care of your health. Most of the time when you go to your doctor, he has an appointment right after you and is doing his best to give enough time to all his patients without them feeling like he's rushing them. You might have the type of doctor who gives you all the time you need but even then, there's only so much he can do in the short time you're there at their office (or doing a virtual call now that the COVID-19 pandemic has changed the entire world).

I went to the doctor because I was complaining about low energy. He explained to me that he had something that would make me a "new man." He explained that after taking it I would be able to gain muscle easier, have more energy, and feel like a completely new person. His solution: a magical testosterone cream. He told me

I had low testosterone and prescribed me a cream as a form of treatment. My wife and I decided to hold off on taking his prescription and decided to do some research of our own.

I ended up finding some natural things to increase my testosterone. A couple of years later I went to another doctor for a checkup and explained to them I wanted to see where my levels were. Their test showed my testosterone levels were high. I told them about my previous experience and out of curiosity they asked me to bring in my old test results for them to look at. This new doctor told me that when I was first tested, my testosterone levels were high back then too.

I'm glad my wife and I decided to do a little research because had I taken the testosterone, as prescribed by the first doctor, my body would have ceased its own production of testosterone and I might have been stuck taking a prescription for the rest of my life that I never needed in the first place. I talk to my doctors because they're the experts, however, I still like learning as much as I can about what I can do to improve my health.

64

DRINK MORE WATER

Drinking water regularly is important for staying healthy. When you don't drink enough water, your brain shrinks. With diseases like Alzheimer's the brain goes from being a grape to a dried-up raisin because of dehydration.[20] Your body is made up of about 60% water. Of that amount you lose about 2-3 liters of water every day just through respiration, sweating, and other normal processes.[21]

An article from Harvard School of Public Health shows the benefits of drinking enough water every day: "Drinking enough water each day is crucial for many reasons: to regulate body temperature, keep joints lubricated, prevent infections, deliver nutrients to cells, and keep organs functioning properly. Being well-hydrated also improves sleep quality, cognition, and mood."[22]

Buy a water bottle (I usually do glass or BPA free), fill it up in the morning with good, clean water, and keep drinking throughout the day. There are a lot of opinions about how much water you should drink a day to stay healthy, but a simple recommendation is to drink enough water to make sure your urine is light-yellow or colorless.[23] You could always fall back on the eight glasses of water a day approach, but each person requires a different amount.

It's probably a struggle but do your best to drink more water and stay healthy.

65

THE BENEFITS OF INTERMITTENT FASTING

Intermittent Fasting can improve your health. But what is it? There are several different ways people use intermittent fasting. The method I was introduced to was where you set a cut-off time at night for when you will stop eating. For me, that time was 9 o'clock. My first meal in the morning would be no earlier than 11 o'clock, giving me fourteen hours of fasting. I then had from 11 am to 9 to get in all three thousand calories for that day.

I decided to try it because I heard it could help you with your blood sugar levels and help you have more energy throughout the day. I was very skeptical of the whole thing, but I decided to try it. For the first time in years, I was able to eat without my blood sugar spiking up and down and feeling like I was going to pass out after every meal.

Following are just a few of the many benefits of intermittent fasting—compliments of Dr. Josh Axe. I recently watched a video by Dr. Axe where he discussed how intermittent fasting can help you to naturally maintain higher levels of HGH (Human Growth Hormone) and even help you maintain higher levels of testosterone, which can be very helpful as you age.[24]

-Helps your waistline (you can trim down)

-Stabilizes blood sugar levels

-Reduces inflammation

-Helps keep your heart healthy

-Protects your brain health[25]

Do some research into intermittent fasting and speak to your doctor to find out if it's safe for your specific situation, and to see if it's something you might benefit from doing. It's not for everyone, but it might be something that helps you. I want to give a shoutout to my brother-in-law, Kenneth, who first told me about it. Once he did, it started me on a journey to find out more for myself.

He wrote a book called, *385,000 Calories Later: How Lost (And Kept Off) 110 Pounds,* which is available on Amazon. In it, he talks about his journey from a childhood struggle with obesity, to becoming a highly trained U.S. Marine Corps Sergeant and eventually crossing over to become a Captain.

Even after being out of the Marines for over a decade, he's still trim, fit, and maintains great health. There's so much information to cover about intermittent fasting. Make it a point to become a student of life and learn as much as you can so you can stay on the path of victory and impact.

66

DON'T JUST SIT THERE

While you're reading this chapter, I could have someone preparing a meal for me, another person driving to my house to drop it off, and all without ever lifting a finger. All I have to do is say a few words and my phone will respond. I don't even have to open my wallet to pay for it. I can just push a button on my phone, and it's done. I could do all of that while sitting on the couch watching TV. If I wanted to, I could buy technology that would allow me to turn my lights on and off without having to get up.

Most of the time I spent writing this book was while sitting. But what would it do to my health if all I ever did was sat at a desk writing, hardly ever got sunshine, and never exercised? In *7 Pillars of Health*, Dr. Colbert explains that when you don't engage in physical activity and lead a sedentary lifestyle, what takes place inside your body is like what happens with water that sits stagnant.

If you've ever passed by a nasty-looking pond, that's a picture of what's going on inside your body when you just sit all the time. Your body is made up of about 60-75% water depending on your age.[26] As Dr. Colbert explains, if that water just sits there and never gets "stirred up" by movement, you'll eventually get sick.

It's almost like you're a cesspool of filth on the inside.[27]

Something my wife's family has taught me is to mix eating with physical activity. For example, if we have a family gathering it's common for us to go on a walk within a few hours of eating. My family and I eat out like anyone else, but we try not to make all the activities we do revolve around eating: that's a recipe for disaster. Exercise and movement are important for maintaining good health. Find ways to incorporate things into your daily routine that will get you moving. Don't neglect this important part of your health.

RESOURCES

Achieving Physical Strength and Stamina

☐ Excellent source for fitness workouts and routines used by martial artists. You'll find beginner to advanced exercises you can modify to fit your own level. Many of them include instructional videos: https://blackbeltwiki.com/martial-arts-physical-fitness

☐ *The Men's Fitness Exercise Bible: 101 Best Workouts to Build Muscle, Burn Fat and Sculpt Your Best Body Ever!* The ultimate resource for working just about every muscle you can think about. You'll find ideas for hitting the weight room, using kettlebells, resistance bands, natural body weight, and much more.

☐ *TB12:* Book by Tom Brady where he shares how to achieve long-term physical fitness and minimize your risk for injury by increasing *pliability* and training smart. Great book with great principles and even includes some nutrition tips.

☐ Nutrition: *The Seven Pillars of Health*: I would highly recommend you read this book if you just want an all-around quick education on nutrition. The author is a doctor who takes complex topics and breaks them down in a way that's simple to understand. If you already know a lot about nutrition, I still recommend this book as a reminder of good habits to keep you on track.

☐ Great articles by James Clear on working out
https://jamesclear.com/exercise-habit
https://jamesclear.com/strength-training

☐ Articles on Staying Hydrated and Drinking Enough Water
https://www.nationalacademies.org/news/2004/02/report-sets-dietary-intake-levels-for-water-salt-and-potassium-to-maintain-health-and-reduce-chronic-disease-risk

☐ Resources on how to Improve the Quality of Your Sleep
https://www.betterhealth.vic.gov.au/health/conditionsandtreatments/sleep-hygiene
https://www.betterhealth.vic.gov.au/health/HealthyLiving/Mood-and-sleep

Sleep Smarter: 21 Proven Tips to Sleep Your Way to a Better Body, Better Health and Bigger Success by Shawn Stevenson

67

ENERGY DRINKS AND HEART ATTACKS

For nearly three years I worked at least ninety hours a week. Many of those days I remember feeling like I was going to fall asleep while driving to work in the mornings. I had no choice but to work, but still, I felt like there was no way I would make it unless I had two or three large cans of energy drinks every day.

After a while I got worried because it felt like every time I went to the bathroom, acid was coming out. I had doctors run tests that showed me I was highly acidic. The level of acidity in my blood was equivalent to what a car battery would be. I was so dehydrated I was destroying my organs one can at a time. The doctor's warning that consuming energy drinks the way I was could eventually cause a heart attack, was enough for me to stop.

After I stopped consuming energy drinks the problem went away, and I was able to get back to normal. My goal is not to tell you to stop drinking energy drinks but rather to encourage you to pay attention to what you're putting into your body and how it's affecting you. It would be better to research healthier or more natural ways you can get caffeine without damaging your long-term health. If you pick up a can and can't pronounce most of the words, it might not be something you want to put in your body.

68

DON'T WAIT FOR THE DOCTOR
TO TELL YOU YOU'RE SICK

Y ou don't have to wait for a doctor to tell you you're sick before you decide to start making better health choices. By that point, you could have health and weight problems that might have been prevented. One of the biggest issues for a lot of people is eating too much sugar.

In 2010 the average American consumed about 60 pounds of high-fructose syrup (HFCS), a sweetener used in a wide range of foods and beverages, including fruit juice, soda, cereal, bread, yogurt, ketchup, and mayonnaise.[28] A study that was conducted by the Princeton Neuroscience Institute reported that the animals tested who had "access to [HFCS] gained 48 percent more weight than those eating a normal diet."[29]

If you look in your refrigerator or food pantries, do you see a lot of foods that have high fructose corn syrup? If so, you could be setting yourself up to struggle with weight gain, cholesterol, diabetes, high blood pressure.[30] I'm not trying to tell you to go out and make some huge health change, I'm only trying to give you the knowledge to help you make more informed decisions.

When you're in the store shopping and you have a decision to choose between something that's made with HFCS corn syrup versus something that's not, what will you do? I eat healthy but I don't get paralyzed by food labels. I'm not a slave to sugar, but I'm also not a slave to a diet.

To help you avoid this sugary mess, I want to make one suggestion. With as many things that have added and unnecessary sugar in them as possible. Instead of using sugar, use honey; try using stevia. I prefer the Trader Joe's brand of Stevia best, but you can't use too much, or else it will turn bitter.

That's ironic, because "Stevias and their related molecules occur naturally in plants and are more than 200 times sweeter than sugar."[31] One of the benefits of stevia is that it can help regulate blood sugar levels. It's shown to help lower high blood sugar levels, yet at the same time doesn't have the same lowering effect on normal levels.[32]

My children enjoy homemade lemonade using stevia and it tastes just as good as it would if it were loaded with a bunch of sugar. You can be creative and find healthier ways to eat what you like. You just have to do your homework. Choose foods that have less sugar.

Choose to take responsibility for your health while it's still in your control. You don't have to wait for a doctor to tell you you're sick before you decide to start taking better care of your health.

69

DON'T STAY UP LATE, IT CAN WAIT

Getting enough sleep could be the difference between success or failure. My mantra used to be "stay up late, it just can't wait!" It was typical for me to go to sleep at 2 or 3 am trying to *finish* what I had left for the day. Then I woke up with very little motivation for the day's tasks, no energy, and even less productivity.

By learning the discipline of going to bed early and waking up well-rested, I've been able to accomplish much more. This might be more difficult depending on your work schedule or situation. But if the only thing standing between you and a good night's rest is procrastination or the distraction of entertainment, consider setting some time limits for yourself. Besides that, getting more sleep is better for your health.

Shawn Stevenson explains that "high quality sleep fortifies your immune system, balances your hormones, boosts your metabolism, increases physical energy, and improves the function of your brain."[33] There are things you can do to improve your sleep, like cutting back on caffeine late in the day, shutting down your electronics a couple of hours before bedtime, and getting in some exercise during the day.[34]

I struggle with this one too, but I reached a point where I got tired of being tired. Something that has helped me recently is planning out how much sleep I'm going to get each night. When I do this, I'll look at my calendar for the week and decide the total amount of sleep I want for the week. Once I do that, I write down what times I'll go to bed and wake up. This gives me something to work for and reminds me how important it is to make sure I'm getting rest. Don't stay up late, it can wait!

70

HEALTHY STRESS RELIEF

Imagine waking up every day with no problems. The weather outside is perfect, all your bills are paid, your kids behave perfectly, you have no health issues, and the only thing that enters your mind are positive thoughts. You're at the top of the ladder when it comes to success, all your relationships are uplifting and fulfilling, and your world is just great.

That sounds too good to be true and it should, because that's nothing but a fairy tale. Life isn't always like that. No matter how much faith you have, how positive you are, or how well things are going in your life, at some point you will get stressed out. How you deal with stress is important.

You can either reach for two inches of nicotine and fill your lungs with poison every time you get stressed out, or you can find a healthy outlet. Don't settle for smoking cigarettes—or anything else that's not good for you, to relieve stress. There are better ways to relieve stress than nicotine. If you don't have a regular stress relief activity or routine you engage in, you probably have no idea what type of damage you're doing to yourself.

Have you ever heard the terms cortisol or adrenal fatigue? These are all words that come up whenever you start talking about stress. Cortisol is a hormone that plays an important role in helping to keep us awake and alert, preventing fatigue and brain fog, allowing us to respond to and escape perceived dangers, and many other important functions.[35]

The problem is that stress contributes to high cortisol production, which is "tied to symptoms and ailments including weight gain, anxiety, sleep disorders, hormonal imbalances and fertility problems, in addition to many other problems.[36] In an earlier chapter, titled "Half-Time," I talked about the need to give yourself a break. The need for stress relief is one of the reasons why.

If you want to have victory and impact, you have to be able to regroup and get away from the everyday responsibilities and stresses of life. When I first joined the military, my superiors would ask me when I was going to take a vacation. That's because I would go the whole year without requesting time off. I told them I wasn't planning on it, but they *made me* take some vacation. Even the Marines take time off. Shouldn't that tell you something?

If you're quick to become irritable, are constantly worried about something, or feel like you're carrying the weight of the world on your shoulders, there are things you can do that will help. I believe there is always a spiritual and mental component to stress but that's not what I'm focusing on here. I'm referring specifically to healthy activities you can do regularly that can help you relieve stress.

One of the things I do to relieve stress and get a good workout is hitting my heavy bag. For you, it might be something different. I know guys who fly drones as one of their outlets. They go outside and just have fun being a kid, flying around a remote-control *toy*.

You could try watching comedy, taking a walk, jogging, bicycling, woodworking projects, or something else that fits you. Whatever you do, find a healthy outlet for stress relief. In the chapter titled, "Start Having Fun Again," I include several ideas for activities you can do. Try one of them out. It's important to find healthy ways to relieve stress.

71

HOW I AVOIDED DIABETES

It saddens me when I see young children who are obese. Many of them even develop diabetes at a young age because of the choices their parents make for themselves and their children. I don't say that to judge or condemn anyone, but the issue seems to be getting worse.

When I was a child, I watched as my dad lay on the couch for days. His health was withering away, but he wouldn't let me call an ambulance for him. Finally, it got so bad he begged me to call the ambulance. The paramedics rushed him to the hospital. After treating him, the doctors explained that had I not called 911 when I did, he would probably have died from a diabetic coma.

Even though most of the time things like diabetes or high cholesterol are associated with people who are overweight, you would be surprised how many people who look healthy still deal with these types of issues. I was one of them.

A few years ago, my doctor handed me a prescription for Metformin, a prescription drug used to help those who have Type II Diabetes. I couldn't believe he was telling me I was a borderline diabetic. How could this even be possible? Just two years earlier I ran three miles in 18:33. I ate fairly healthy, was in great shape, and was nowhere close to being overweight.

The National Diabetes Statistics Report in 2020 showed that 89% of the over 34 million people who had diabetes, were linked with being overweight or obese.[37] This situation drove me to start searching for reasons behind what was going on. I was shocked at what I found out.

For years I had a Vitamin D deficiency. I learned that Vitamin D deficiency could increase my chances of having Type II Diabetes. There are all types of studies out there and some doctors don't agree about whether it does or not. All I can say is that after working to increase my Vitamin D, I had no sign of Type II Diabetes.

An article from Grassroots Health perfectly describes my situation: Once I knew I was on the path to diabetes, I started focusing on "lifestyle changes, such as diet, exercise, and increasing vitamin D levels to 40-60 ng/ml (100-150 nmol/L), which can help prevent, or even reverse, prediabetes."[38] I also continued to work out, cut back on sugar, and eat more fruits and vegetables.

I'm at a much higher risk for diabetes because of my family history, but I didn't want to live with something I could avoid. I took steps to change the direction of my health and I want to encourage you to do what you can to avoid these types of issues while you still can.

If that means changing your diet, taking vitamin and mineral supplements, getting a personal trainer, do what you need to do. I encourage you to seek professional medical advice and make informed decisions to stay healthy.

72

COMPETITION BETWEEN CONVENIENCE AND HEALTH

When it comes to making healthy choices about what to eat, most people know that fast food isn't always the best route to go. For a lot of people, convenience works better. Between busy work schedules, lack of energy to cook fresh meals, and even limitations on cash, there are a lot of reasons why people choose convenience over health.

There was a time before I got married when I ate over $400 in fast food every month. I remember standing in line at my favorite restaurant and seeing the number of calories that were in one burger: over 1,300, but I didn't care. With how busy I was, I thought it was just easier for me to live life off burgers, fries, tacos, pizza, and all the other greasy goodies I could get my hands on.

I acted like this was my only option. Every now and then I'd cook rice, bake chicken, and throw in some canned vegetables. I'm grateful for how much I've learned from my wife and the rest of her family about nutrition. If you're struggling to get yourself on track as far as eating right, I want to give you a few tips that might help you set yourself up for success.

I eat a mostly plant-based diet, which turns a lot of guys off. I was one of them, but a few years before writing this book I struggled with so many health issues after getting out of the military, I felt like I was dying. I looked healthy on the outside, but I was quickly declining. My wife and I did a lot of research into what we could do to get our family's health to a better level.

We already ate somewhat healthy, but our diet still had room for improvement. I wanted to eat more fruits and vegetables, but I was hesitant because I didn't want to lose weight. I thought, "How in the world am I going to live without meat?" I busted my myth a few months ago. I was able to gain eight pounds of lean muscle in about two months, while still doing a lot of cardio. I got plenty of protein, calcium, and never felt deprived.

The way I approach eating is that I can eat whatever I want to. I never feel deprived or like I *can't* do something. I just *choose* to eat healthier, but if I feel like eating a pizza, that's what I do. I just don't make it a lifestyle. I think most people would benefit from doing the same.

There's so much that could be shared on this topic, but for now, my primary goal is to help you think about some ways you can make it easier for you to break free from the fast-food cycle should you decide to stick with it. Here are a few things you might want to consider buying:

1. Insulated lunch bag backpack

2. Reusable Ice/Freezer Packs for Coolers and Lunch bags: this one is self-explanatory, but just make sure you buy enough to keep your food or beverages at a cool enough temp. Use this to keep the food inside your lunch bag cold.

3. Crock-Pot: you don't have to be a chef to make good meals. Get a crock-pot, throw in some organic chicken, vegetables (onions, celery, etc.), and you have a main dish. Use your

crock-pot to make beans (black, kidney, etc.). A pot can last you a long time. Whatever you don't use right away, just freeze in a good sealable container.

4. Sealable Tupperware/Ziploc-Type Containers: get a set of these that has multiple sizes. I prefer glass but use plastic as well. Use these to store snacks or to separate different parts of your meals.

5. Rice Cooker: this will make life easier for you but isn't necessary. You can always just use the stove.

6. Fruit: you can add fruit to your lunch bag in place of candy or other sugary foods.

7. Blender: I have a Ninja and it works well for everything we need in our house. We make a ton of smoothies, and this has worked well for us. I've heard Vitamix is a good product too, but it will cost you at least two or three hundred dollars. You don't have to spend unnecessary money on meal replacement protein bars: just make a smoothie that's loaded with calories and a lot of nutrition.

8. Ziploc/Freezer bags: We keep these bags on hand in one gallon and quart sizes. If you're going to eat healthier it will help to have these. I make what I call power packs. I'll put oranges, apples, and grapes into a gallon bag. Then I'll have another bag with carrots, bell peppers, and a container with hummus. I'll use another bag for cashews or almonds. These are all snacks. If you had to describe what you would currently put in your bag, would it consist of cookies and candy bars? If so, consider replacing it with a healthier option.

I'm not a nutritionist or health professional. I'm just sharing what works for me. There's a lot to share on this topic, but I hope you stay informed by doing your own research, along with talking to your doctor or nutritionist to come up with a plan that fits your needs.

73

DECLUTTER FOR SUCCESS AND MENTAL CLARITY

I knew someone who kept unopened QVC boxes in her living room stacked almost to the ceiling. She was a clean person but every time I walked into her house, I felt like I was trapped. I didn't think about stuff like that back then, but all the clutter in her house was a fire hazard.

You couldn't see the floors and walls. Nobody went into the living room. It was kinda cool though because there were a lot of times where she would grab something and give it to me as a gift. It was like she had a little store in her house. That might have worked for her, but in most cases, a cluttered environment can affect your mental state.

You might be used to working with a bunch of clutter everywhere, but if you are, you're taking away from your ability to focus and not be distracted by all the things your brain is trying to process and make sense of. I have a bad habit of collecting paperwork.

When my wife and I first got married, I brought along two large storage bins full of documents that took us hours to shred. Every time my wife would ask if we were finished, I'd reach into the bin and pull out another stack of hundreds of sheets of paper. Every few months I have to spend the afternoon decluttering. It drives my wife crazy, and I can hardly concentrate either.

"Cluttered spaces can have negative effects on our stress and anxiety levels, as well as our ability to focus, our eating choices, and even our sleep."[39] You'll also waste unnecessary time trying to find things you need and then end up frustrated. It's important to keep your physical environment clean and uncluttered. If you haven't been in the habit of doing this, set your stopwatch and take five minutes and declutter.

74

DON'T LET HURT BECOME POISON

The hurt you experience can easily become poisonous, turning into anger, bitterness, and resentment. It's easy to hold a grudge against someone, but it's not easy to hold a grudge against someone without destroying yourself. Even if you look strong, you're like a tree that's rotting on the inside.

While running on a trail one day I approached a tree that had fallen over. It was one of the biggest trees in the entire park and I found it hard to believe something so large had fallen, while all the smaller trees around it didn't. I discovered the problem: the tree looked good on the outside, but it had been slowly rotting on the inside.

Sometimes people can say and do things to you that hurt and leave you confused. This can be even more devastating—especially when someone close to you does this. You can try and act like you're strong on the outside, like everything is okay, but if you don't deal with what's going on inside of you, you'll end up rotting away—not just mentally and emotionally, but also physically.

There's so much more that can be said about this topic, but I just want to lead you toward what I believe is the first big step in your healing process: forgiveness. Why start here? Because forgiveness is like medicine for the body and soul. "It engages the parasympathetic nervous system, which helps your immune system function more efficiently and makes room for feel-good hormones [your body naturally produces on its own] like serotonin and oxytocin."[40]

Your act of forgiveness frees you to be happier because you release the negative emotions of anger and bitterness. If you're struggling in this area, it might be helpful to seek out professional counseling. You don't have to spend the rest of your life allowing your hurt to become poison. Your healing might not be an easy process, but it's worth it. Life is too short!

75

ARE YOU SURE YOU SHOULD DO THAT?

Sometimes the path to victory comes by slowing down, backing away from a situation, and not making a decision you might later regret. That's not always easy; I know this from firsthand experience. This is something I've struggled with over the years. I can't tell you how many times I sent an email I should have waited to send or shot off a text message I would later regret.

It's like opening the radiator cap on a car when the engine is hot: you can cause a lot of damage. In some cases, you can even get 3rd-degree burns that will leave scars and cost more than it was worth. If you wait until the engine cools down and then release the cap, you're going to have a much better outcome.

The next time you're in a situation where you're revved up, decide now that you will do nothing in that moment. Have someone you can call who will honestly ask you, "Are you sure you should do that?" It should be someone you respect and trust who can be a listening ear and help you buy some time to cool off and get into a better state of mind. Do today what you won't regret tomorrow.

76

ALCOHOL CAN CLOUD YOUR JUDGMENT

One moment of insobriety can flip your entire life (or someone else's) upside down. Some of the worst decisions ever made were by good people who were not sober. I saw this story play out in my dad's life. He told me of the day he found out his son was killed in an accident by a man who was drunk while driving an 18-wheeler. I'm sure that driver would probably never think of taking the life of an innocent five-year-old, but that's exactly what he ended up doing.

My dad hit a downward spiral after that and began turning to drugs and alcohol to help numb the pain of what he was going through. All it took was just *one* decision by that drunk driver to ruin so many lives. I remember my dad opening up to me when I got older about the pain he went through all those years. I can relate to the temptation to turn to alcohol to cope with life's pain.

In my early twenties, I dealt with depression and during those times I frequently had the thought that if I just drank, somehow things would seem better. I learned some valuable lessons from other people's experiences, and I didn't want their stories to end up being mine. Because of that, anytime I reached a low point, I made a conscious decision to stay away from it.

Unfortunately, for many people, that's not their story; they ended up turning to alcohol or drugs in hopes of finding relief, only to end up in regretful situations. While studying for my master's degree in counseling I had to observe AA meetings. I found that my past thoughts and emotions of wanting to turn to alcohol to *relieve my pain* weren't too different than what many of those alcoholics were going through.

It's only by God's grace I made the decision back then not to drink as a way to cope with life's challenges like they did. Commercial advertisements celebrate alcohol yet fail to talk about the devastating effects it has on people's lives. Several other arguments can be made as to why you should remain sober, but my plea to you is to not allow yourself to get trapped up in an alcohol or drug habit that leaves a trail of devastation you can't undo after you've laid it. Stay sober.

Part Eight

TIPS FOR A GREAT MARRIAGE

77

FOR THE UNMARRIED:
STOP LOOKING FOR LOVE

This section isn't just for those who are married. If you're not married yet and are trying to prepare yourself to be ready for this big commitment, don't skip over this section. It's tough being single when you want to be married. There were plenty of times I went to the movies by myself, ate dinner alone, and watched as a husband and wife walked by holding hands.

I knew it would be hard to find the type of woman I wanted, but I was willing to wait on what God had in store for me. It took a lot to say no to the temporary fix of just having a woman to spend time with who I knew I had no intentions of ever marrying. There were many weekend nights I burned a lot of gas. I would drive my car up and down the highway alone while listening to Christian music.

I chose to be lonely and wait on the wife God had for me, instead of trying to make things happen on my own. At one point I even tried a dating site: Christian Mingle. After a few weeks, someone posted a comment that said they were getting rid of their account, and they decided to just trust God to bring them the person He wanted for them. After reading that I was motivated to do the same. I got rid of that account and never looked back.

When you *stop* looking for love, it will find you. If you haven't found that special *one,* stop looking for her. Start working on yourself. Get your finances right, learn how to be a better communicator, study about being a husband, stay focused on your mission.

The moment you least expect it is when it will come. That doesn't mean the woman of your dreams will just come knocking on your door one day. It means you should stop trying so hard to *make* something work and allow *God* to give you the woman He wants for you.

REFLECTION EXERCISE

1. Describe the qualities you desire in your future wife (her personality, how she looks)

2. List what values are important to you that you desire your future wife to have (religious, beliefs about child-rearing, handling money, employment, etc.)

3. Do you completely trust God to send your wife? If not, write why (Ex: "I'm afraid He might not give me the type of woman I want")

4. Pray over this list and ask God to help you trust Him more and to bring you the wife He desires for you.

78

DON'T LEAVE THE DOOR OPEN

One morning my daughter was in her highchair enjoying breakfast when my wife noticed that her eyes got big. She pointed and calmly said, "Look Mom, there's a snake." At first, my wife just smiled, nodded, and kept on with what she was doing until my daughter repeated the same things several times. When my wife finally went to look at what my daughter was pointing at, she saw a snake that was easily six feet in length. And it was crawling up the steps leading to my back door.

I was at work at the time and when my wife called, I could sense something was wrong by the tone of her voice. I let my boss know I needed to leave early, but before I got home, I wanted to make sure I had the tools I needed to take care of this situation if I needed to, so I stopped by the home improvement store and bought the longest shovel I could find. If I was going to deal with a man-eating snake, I wanted to make sure I was ready.

By the time I got home, that thing was gone. None of us ever saw that snake again, but it was probably because I put out twenty pounds of mothballs. The smell was so strong I could hardly stand to go outside the house for a few weeks. So, what does a snake trying to get into my house have to do with having a good marriage?

Everything. Imagine if my wife would have just had the door open that morning. Anything could have come in, including that snake. The same goes for your marriage. Don't leave the door open and make yourself an easy target for things that can come in and destroy your marriage.

One way you can do this is by not allowing yourself to flirt with other women besides your wife. Over the years I've done my best not to ride in the same car alone or have meals alone with women outside my family. Some might think it's too strict, but I would rather stay happily married than allow myself to be caught up in a regretful situation.

Prevention is a great cure. If you're being drawn away by anything that will lure you into cheating on your wife, let it go and chop off any ties with it. Enjoy great sex with your wife, connect spiritually by having times where you pray, read books on marriage, and continue to do everything you can to invest in your marriage.

There are a lot of snakes out there that are just waiting to get into your marriage and wreak havoc. Don't leave the door open.

79

DON'T TEAR EACH OTHER DOWN

Before publishing this book, I either personally spoke to, or know of several women who were interested to know what one guy would tell another guy. Other women will buy this book so they can give to their husband. If you're a woman reading this book you should know that when you make critical comments to your husband, you are chipping away at his honor and respect.

You are setting yourself up as an enemy rather than an ally. He may never admit this, but I just want you to understand something. When you tear your husband down, he'll stop caring about what you have to say. You'll never get the type of response out of him you want.

Have you ever seen a toddler trying to open a bottle that has a childproof cap? What happens? After spinning the cap around several times, they might try to bite it off, step on it, or even throw it. The result is the same. They get nowhere. When you nag your husband, you're no different than that toddler who's trying hopelessly to pry that bottle open.

Your efforts won't work, and you'll just keep getting more and more frustrated. When you tear your husband down, the response you get will be negative, rather than producing the positive outcome you desire. The ironic thing is that even though you might have some valid concerns, nagging combined with a negative tone of voice will work against you.

In the book, *Verbal Judo,* George Thompson said "tone of voice has caused more violence, more divorce, more lost court cases, more lost business, and more brawls than anything else [he could think of]."[41] Likewise, if you're a man who tears down his wife, you'll never have a satisfying relationship until you change.

The two of you will continue to fight and argue, or your wife will walk away quietly keeping in all the hurt you've dished out at her. Your wife will either "bark" back or just choose to withhold her best self from you. One of the keys to a great marriage is not tearing down your wife, especially in front of other people.

If you have failed in this area, try to find a way to do something in front of her coworkers or friends that makes her feel special. Make a sincere apology publicly if you need to. Have flowers delivered to her when her friends are around and make sure there's a nice note in there. The bottom line is that you can't tear your wife down and expect your marriage to be built up.

80

KNOW YOUR WIFE'S LOVE LANGUAGE

Thanks for unloading the dishwasher Honey! Those are six words I love to hear. My wife is a busy mother with two children she homeschools, is a full-time wife and mom, and is even working on starting her own business. Anytime I do something that makes her day a little easier, she is very appreciative of it. I also know her "Love Language" is acts of service.

What makes her feel loved the most is when I *do* things for her. Because I'm aware of my wife's "Love Language, I make it a point to do things I know will give her a deep sense of satisfaction in knowing her husband loves her. Nobody told me before I got married that if I wanted to make my wife feel loved I should unload the dishwasher. We had to learn these things together. I recommend you read *The Five Love Languages* by Gary Chapman.

If you don't want to wait until you read the book, he also has a test available online for couples where you can find out each of your "Love Languages." There's an old saying I used to hear when I worked in recruiting: "Don't confuse effort with effectiveness." The same thing can happen in a marriage.

You can feel like you're doing everything you can to make sure your wife is taken care of. You even surprise her with flowers and presents on your way home several times a month, yet you're surprised to hear that she feels like something is still lacking in your relationship. In other words, your efforts haven't been effective.

Have you ever had a time when your back was itching, and you asked someone to scratch it? What did you do? More than likely, you pointed out for them exactly where you needed them to scratch. Why? Because you have a need. They could scratch every area of your back and never touch the one spot that needed it the most. They've done a lot of work and you appreciate it, but there's still an unmet need.

The same can happen in your attempts to be a loving husband. You can feel like you're doing all you can to be a good husband to your wife, yet you sense that she's not happy. It's possible you could be doing all the right things yet your wife still needs something more, but for most guys, this isn't the case.

Stop scratching around the itch and find out exactly what you need to focus on to make your wife happy. Don't let all your efforts go toward everything else except the *one* thing your wife longs for. She might long to spend time with you yet the only thing you focus on is buying her nice things.

Will she appreciate your hard work and the nice things you give her? Of course, but she'll still have that part of her that's lacking. Make a point to find out your wife's love language and shower her with it. Following are three questions I came across in college you can start with that will help you get pointed in the right direction.

REFLECTION QUESTIONS

1. What are three things you would like me to do more of?

2. What are three things you would like me to do less of?

3. What can we do to connect on a deeper level?

81

PROTECT YOUR HOME

As a man, one of the greatest burdens I carry is the responsibility I have of protecting my family. It's something I take very seriously. I'm generally a very easy-going guy but I don't play around when it comes to my family's safety. You probably feel that same sense of responsibility.

I know guys who hardly thought about owning a weapon until they got married and had children. Many of them have gone through training and met the legal requirements to be able to own and carry firearms. Others take up boxing or self-defense training and work toward becoming black belts.

As men, that's what we do. We protect the ones we love! If you're like me, your most sincere prayer is that you *never* have to use force against a burglar who breaks into your home or someone who tries to harm your family. You might even have an alarm system with cameras around your house to deter someone from wanting to target you. All these things are great, but there's still one thief that can easily creep into your home: negativity.

After having a rough day at work it's easy to allow all the negative things you experience to creep into your home. It's easy to allow other people's actions and bad attitudes to rub off on you. Don't let others rob your family of the peace you should have. Decide you won't dwell on all the bad things people say and do. Protect your home from this unwelcome thief that will steal time away from what you should be doing: enjoying the moments you have with your family. Protect your home.

82

WHOSE MONEY IS IT?

You're married and have no money problems. If you wanted to go out today and buy a luxury car with cash, you could. You have enough money saved up for all your children to go to college. You can afford to hire a chef and a maid to make things easier around the house.

The amount you give to charity each year is larger than most people make for the entire year. You have several accountants and financial advisors who help you keep track of all your assets. You and your wife hardly ever have conversations about money. Okay, so that probably doesn't describe you, but like one of my friends says, "Why couldn't it?"

Sorry, I got off track for a moment, let's get back to business. No matter how much money you have coming in, there is a need for you and your wife to work together to handle your finances properly. I've heard so many people over the years ask questions like, "Who's money is it?" "Who's in charge of it?"

Each couple handles things differently, but here's what's worked for my wife and me. We believe God ultimately blesses us with any money that flows into our house. Everything we make belongs to both of us and goes into one big pot. Something that's worked well for us is that once we pay our tithes, all our bills are paid, money is put in savings, and all the other miscellaneous expenses are taken care of, we each would have our own spending money to use for eating out or buying whatever we wanted.

We each got the same amount, and it would increase or decrease according to how much we could afford. When it came to spending larger amounts of money, we made an agreement that we would talk with each other before we spent anything over $50. That was the amount we started at when we first got married.

There were many times I was in a store and wanted to buy something I didn't need but because of our agreement, I would call my wife and talk it over. She would talk some sense into me, and I would thank her for helping me stay on track. As time progressed, we moved that limit to $200.

We allowed ourselves to be accountable to each other so we could both reach the same goal of staying financially stable. What about when one person is a spender, and the other person likes saving? That's what the allowance I mentioned earlier is for. The spender can spend his allowance and the saver can save hers.

You have the agreement in place that you won't spend over a certain dollar amount, all the bills are taken care of. What else is there to do? It might be helpful to give more control over what gets spent to the one who's more cost-conscious or good at handling administrative things like making sure things get paid on time.

To help you with this, you could always set up as many payments as possible to come out of your paycheck automatically. Do what works best for your situation. Decide that you're going to work together and not allow money, or the lack of it to ruin your marriage.

REFLECTION QUESTIONS

1. Do you have healthy conversations about money?

2. Do you have a good system to make sure you stay within your financial means?

3. Are you working together toward a common goal? Is there room for improvement in what you're doing to get there?

83

DON'T LET PORNOGRAPHY RUIN YOUR MARRIAGE

My dad was diagnosed with terminal cancer, and I didn't find out until months later when he only had days to live. My phone rang and one of my uncles was on the other end: "Dak, I have something to tell you. Your father is very sick, and the doctors are saying he only has days to live."

I flew out to see him the next day and spent ten days by his side, of which I only left twice. Here I was in what felt like the darkest moment of my life, watching my hero wither away, and there was nothing I could do about it. Was he a perfect man? No, but he was my hero.

I would soon come face-to-face with my own imperfections. What had been a vice of my past became a thing of the present. I began to turn to pornography to cope with the pain and depression I was experiencing from losing my dad. Before long I felt guilty about it and knew I had to come clean, but I faced yet another challenge: who was I supposed to talk to about this?

I was supposed to be someone who had it together, a churchgoer, someone who lived right. My and wife and I had only been married a little over two years when all of this happened. She respected me and treated me like a king, and I just couldn't go on knowing I was living like this; I loved her too much to do that. I took the first step and fessed up about what I was doing.

I knew beforehand that I could face shame and embarrassment if my family and friends knew about my struggles, but it was more important to me to get things right and put this in the past. At least that's what I was hoping would happen. When I broke the news to her, she paused, took a deep breath, and with the most soul-piercing look, asked, "Why?"

After what felt like the longest pause ever, I expressed to her what I was going through. She told me how thankful she was that I took the step to come to her about what was happening. She explained she was hurt by it, but that what made things easier was that I came to her and confessed it, instead of her having to find out about it on her own. She forgave me and never brought it back up again.

That, coupled with the fact that everything was out in the open, was enough to keep me from going back to it. But that still was only half the battle. What about my heart? I had a bunch of rules in place to make sure this didn't happen again, but I needed to be freed in my heart. For years I didn't even own a smartphone.

I was the guy who got teased for being stuck in another decade because I carried a flip phone. I never used the Internet unless my wife was home. There were even times where my wife needed me to look something up online and asked if I could do it while she was on the phone. I even refused to do that. It took more than rules for me to be freed in my heart.

A few years later, I gave my heart to Christ, and He set me free from even the desire to have this in my life. I was exposed to pornography as a seven or eight-year-old boy while up late one night flipping through cable channels at my cousin's house, but there was something about giving my life to Christ that made me new and free from being drawn to this anymore.

I've had a smartphone for years and haven't looked at pornography once. I realize that not all men struggle with this, but for those who do, there's hope. When faced with difficulty, some turn to alcohol, others to drugs, my way of coping, if left unchecked could have been just as devastating as any of those other addictions had it continued.

If this is something you struggle with, you might be tempted to just keep it a secret, because people respect you and you fear being looked down on. I faced that same pressure; people looked up to me and my family and it wasn't an easy thing for me to come to my wife for help. Like you, I thought about all the things that could go wrong. If you feel like there's no one you can talk to about this, I'm sorry.

Don't let fear of how things will go if you come clean about this keep you from seeking help. Every situation is different. You might feel more comfortable seeking help privately instead of going to your wife. That's okay, just don't make any excuses for staying in the dark and living a defeated life.

You're better than that! You're a man of courage who wants to take a step toward restoring your integrity and fighting for your marriage. Please, get help! I don't even want to imagine how things would be for me today if I would have just continued down that same path. Because I had the courage to take that step, my wife and I enjoy a guilt-free, trusting relationship.

We've been married for almost ten years and no matter how rough our day is, at night—without fail—we always laugh together. We have a great friendship and do just about everything together. All our children know is a mom and dad who's always hugging and smooching.

I already know some guys will read this and think I'm crazy. I used to be one of them. Porn is not just some innocent, harmless thing; it damages lives. By consuming pornography you're supporting an industry that is part of the human and sex trafficking problem. Those who perform these things "are frequently victims of violence, coercion, and drug abuse."[42] The following statistics from Covenant Eyes will give you a glimpse of just how destructive this industry is.

PORNOGRAPHY STATISTICS

- 68% of divorce cases involved one party meeting a new lover over the Internet.
- 56% [of divorce cases] involved one party having "an obsessive interest in pornographic websites."
- 88% of scenes in porn films contain acts of physical aggression, and 49% of scenes contain verbal aggression.
- Only 7% of pastors report their church has a ministry program for those struggling with porn.
- 1 in 5 mobile searches is for pornography.
- $3,075.64 is spent on porn every second on the Internet. Just to give you some perspective, that equals over eleven million dollars per hour.
- 64% of Christian men and 15% of Christian women say they watch porn at least once a month.[43]

In the movie *Fireproof*, the main character is a firefighter who struggles with a pornography addiction, and as a result, his marriage suffers. During a phone conversation, he talks about how the newspaper called twice wanting to interview him for saving someone's life.

He's confused and expresses hurt because he feels like everyone else sees him as a hero except for his wife. One of his coworkers from the fire department challenges him and asks, "You're going to walk into a burning building to save people you don't even know, but you're going to let your own marriage burn to the ground?[44]

The good news is that he didn't and I'm confident that you won't either. I want to thank my wife who fully supports my decision to share this story. We both know that this is something a lot of men struggle with in secret, and we hope our experience will give them the courage to rise up against it, come clean, get help, and gain victory. This is something we all have to be on the guard against. Don't let pornography (or anything else for that matter) ruin your marriage.

Following are some resources that can help you get started toward breaking free from this sin. Look, it wasn't easy for me to write about this, just like it wasn't easy for me to approach my wife and come clean about what I'd been doing. If I can do it, you can too! If you bought this book and are reading this, consider this your opportunity to "face the wind," as we discussed in chapter one. It's time to step up!

RESOURCES TO OVERCOME PORNOGRAPHY ADDICTION

-Article addressing the danger pornography poses to a marriage:
https://www.focusonthefamily.com/marriage/how-pornography-prevents-intimacy-in-your-marriage/

-Get Free eBook! *Your Brain on Porn.* This book helps you understand how porn warps your brain and what you can do about it:
https://learn.covenanteyes.com/your-brain-on-porn-1/

-Celebrate Recovery: A Christ-centered 12-step program aimed at helping you find freedom from hurts, hangups, and habits. It's not a replacement for counseling and therapy but they help people who are struggling with anger, gambling addiction, sexual addiction, and chemical dependency. To find one near you, go to this site:
https://locator.crgroups.info/

-Porn blocking software:
https://www.netnanny.com/features/porn-blocking/
https://www.covenanteyes.com/

-Video of a man who almost ruined his marriage but was able to recover:
https://fightthenewdrug.org/media/travis-and-emilys-story/

-Stories of hope to help you break free from porn:
https://www.blazinggrace.org/what-to-do-to-break-free-from-sexual-sin/
https://www1.cbn.com/can-i-break-addiction-pornography

-Inspirational movie of a man whose marriage was falling apart due to pornography addiction who got a breakthrough and turned things around:
http://www.kendrickbrotherscatalogue.com/fireproof/

84

PROBLEMS AREN'T THE PROBLEM

Problems aren't the problem—every marriage has them. The real issue is not knowing how to properly handle them when they come. My wife and I were blessed to have someone to mentor us for an entire year before we got married. During that time, he showed us what to do when we had a disagreement. He helped us prepare for the inevitable—marriage problems.

A few years ago, I was in a store and heard a guy ask his wife to put something in their cart for him. To me, it seemed like a simple request, but by the tone of her voice, it seemed like she was ready to run him over with the shopping cart. I could tell they had some unresolved issues.

All he did was ask for a pack of food—with not even an ounce of attitude—and she nearly *ripped* his head off. From an outside perspective, it didn't seem like something that should have been that big of a deal. Unfortunately, that's what happens when couples don't know how to resolve their problems.

They carry hurt and resentment around and end up miserable. If you're newly married or are experiencing these types of issues let me give you some comfort. My wife and I experienced this during our first year of marriage, even with all the mentoring we had. It's just inevitable. Even though we had a beautiful wedding ceremony, what helped us is that we spent more time preparing for our marriage than we did for our wedding day.

It's never too late to learn how to start handling your problems better. Although I have a master's degree in Marriage and Family Therapy and have been married for nearly ten years, I make absolutely no claim of being a marriage expert, but I've enjoyed such a great marriage that my wife's name is programmed in my phone as "Heaven on Earth."

Something that has helped my wife and I is that even when we mess up or have disagreements, we both genuinely want to make things right. We both have that trust that the other person has good intentions. If every time you or your wife messes up you assume the worse, then it will be hard to move on and forgive one another.

When you hear the words, "We need to talk," does your relationship take a downward turn for days or weeks? Does it seem like your wife gets defensive every time you try to bring something up to her? How about you? Do you hate when she brings up a problem she has: your relationship is filled with tension, and you can never seem to get your point across? Here are a few basic recommendations that might help you.

Keep a saltshaker nearby. I know. You probably think I'm crazy but hear me out. My wife and I met a gentleman who told us to agree that we would stick it out for sixty years and then see what happens from there. He also told us anytime we had a disagreement we should grab a saltshaker.

We would each take turns expressing everything we want to say. The person holding the saltshaker gets to speak freely, without interruption (at least that's the plan), while the other one talks. At no point do you interrupt the other person.

If you're the one listening, this can get challenging because instead of paying attention, you can find yourself thinking of everything you want to say to respond to what you're hearing. If you feel necessary, grab a sheet of paper, and write down what you hear your spouse say.

Even if it hurts to hear, there's probably *some* amount of truth in it. The best thing you can do is try to remain calm and try not to lash back out at everything you disagree with. The goal is to hear each other out as respectfully as possible and try to come to a solution together. Remember, you're on the same team.

This isn't a book exclusively on marriage or else I would delve deeper into this topic, but you should check out a book by Dr. Henry Cloud called *How to Have That Difficult Conversation.* You and your wife should both read it, take notes, and apply it as much as possible.

If necessary, seek a good pastor/marriage counselor who can point you in the right direction and give you some tools to help you learn how to better work through problems together. It might also be helpful for you to read books on how to increase your emotional intelligence. Do everything you can to build a great marriage.

85

DAD, LEADER, OR BOSS?

Does your wife want a dad, a leader, or a boss? Over the years I've worked with guys who come to work and beat their chest saying things like: "I run things in my house;" "My wife knows who's in charge." I wonder what type of marriage that makes for? One where the husband bosses his wife around like an employee. Just a word of advice, your wife is not your employee. She's a queen that should be treated as such.

Am I saying you should be a "yes man?" Not at all! That's a recipe for disaster too. Your wife doesn't need a boss, she needs a good leader. Even if you have a strong wife, she needs someone who can be a leader, not just someone who goes along with everything she says. She needs you to step up and be a leader in your finances, in your spiritual and physical health, and other areas.

You might be a guy who's a great leader and doesn't lead by being demanding, but you treat your wife like she's your child. This can happen, especially if you're several years older than your wife. Whenever something happens you go into mentorship and teaching mode, when all your wife wants is a husband to listen to her.

You treat her like she needs guidance to make every little decision. She's *choking* and needs to be able to breathe a little without feeling like she can hardly do anything without your permission. By no means do I consider myself a great leader, or the ideal husband (whatever that is).

I mess up all the time, but what I can say is that my wife is happy, and she will do almost anything I ask her to. One of the greatest reasons for that is that although I'm not perfect, I have a track record of wanting to follow God, love my family, and do what's right.

She knows that I seek God for decisions that need to be made and that our marriage is a team effort. Are you the guy sitting there with your arms crossed, watching TV while your wife is struggling with the kids and other responsibilities, or are you a leader who's not afraid to come alongside your wife and work as a team?

Your wife will appreciate you leading her without making her feel like she's one of your employees or like she's a child. As men, we are challenged with the important task of leading our families. Let's commit ourselves to doing our best to do it well.

Part Nine

REACHING YOUR FULL POTENTIAL

86

THE POWER OF JOURNALING

Journaling is a habit that can benefit you in a lot of ways. I've been journaling on and off for over fifteen years and have used it for business planning, Bible study and sermon notes, writing down awesome things that have happened in my life and the lives of family and friends, and keeping track of my hobbies. I use a prayer journal, where I track answers to prayers. I've used journaling for just getting out thoughts that were bottled up inside that I just needed to let go of.

One of the greatest benefits I've found from journaling is that it gives me something positive to reflect on. Sometimes I flip through old journals and think back on past victories, reflect on areas where I've grown, goals I've accomplished, and even reflect on tough times I went through. Now I just make it a part of my morning routine.

Following is a sample journal to help you get started. If you noticed, throughout this book I've given you reflection exercises. If you've been completing them, you started journaling already. I've also made a workbook that goes along with this book that has all the reflection questions and exercises in one place.

I also included some extra material that you might find helpful as you try to apply some of the things discussed in this book. If you would like a copy, visit: <u>habitsforgrowth.com/bonus101</u>.

JOURNAL

1. What went well this week? What brought a smile to your face?

2. What could have been better this week?

3. What changes do I need to make?

87

EVERY MAN NEEDS A MENTOR

Each of my brothers is over 6'2" tall. I tapped out at 5'8," and I'm okay with that: I don't have to pay as much for shoes and clothes as they do. But my brothers aren't just physically tall, they are men of great character. Unfortunately, broken homes and a lack of positive male role models are becoming more rampant.

Before I continue, I want to say this though. It seems like there is a lot more news coverage of the things that men *aren't* doing right than there are of the great things that *are* happening. Nevertheless, way too many men grow up without the type of direction and guidance they need in life. I would have been one of them if it weren't for my brother.

After graduating high school my brother had a world of opportunities in front of him. He grew up playing basketball with guys who are in the NBA. He had opportunities to even travel overseas to start a career. At one point he was even invited to model for a celebrity. He chose to turn down all those opportunities instead, to help my mom raise me. He realized my need for a positive male role model and stepped up to the plate.

I needed someone who could be an example for me of what it meant to be a man. As a "know-it-all" teenager, I laughed at him when he tried to give me advice. Little did he know, I was latching on to bits and pieces of the knowledge and wisdom he was trying to pour into me.

As I got older, I realized that my need for a mentor never stopped. Growing up I didn't see an example of what made a good husband or dad. When I became an adult, I was blessed to be surrounded by men who had a genuine love for God and their families. These were men with imperfections like anyone else, but to me, they are heroes. They are hard-working men of character and integrity.

If you have been trying to do life on your own without any positive examples in your life, it's time to find someone who can pour into you. Even if you think you got it all figured out—you're in the "pros," you still need a man. Even professional athletes embrace this concept. Many of them have personal trainers, mentors, and coaches who help them go beyond where they would on their own.

Hard work and talent are great, but sometimes you need someone to help you harness all of that so you can experience the greatest level of victory and impact possible. Have you ever had someone like this to help you grow? A mentor or coach? If not, you haven't even begun tapping into your full potential. Every man needs a mentor.

88

THERE'S ALWAYS ROOM FOR IMPROVEMENT

You don't get better by asking what's right, you get better by asking what's wrong. There's *always* room for improvement. Don't ask how good are we doing? Ask, what can we do to improve? If you never take time to see where you can do better, you'll become disillusioned when the results don't come.

You'll work harder and pray harder, only to find that you experience no lasting change. Sometimes the change that needs to happen will only be visible to an outsider. Ask people for honest feedback without you becoming defensive. Once you get it, examine it, and take the necessary actions.

This doesn't mean you have to go digging up things to fix. Just don't be afraid to make changes when needed. Unfortunately, not everyone's feedback will seem positive or even constructive, but it's still important to know where you can make improvements at.

Getting feedback from someone you trust who will be truthful with you without trying to tear you down, might be the best thing you can do. Another approach you could try is taking assessments. The LifeScore™ Assessment by Michael Hyatt is a great place to start. There are plenty of other assessments you can take, but this is one I like because it covers a lot of different areas. Before you continue to the next chapter, visit habitsforgrowth.com/bonus101 to get more helpful tools and resources, along with bonus material that will help you as you seek to improve.

89

BECOME A LIFELONG LEARNER

S omething I've noticed about the most successful people I come across is they have an interest in learning and reading. They understand that one of the biggest benefits of reading is that it allows you to tap into other people's experiences. There's a book out there for just about anything you can think of.

If there's something you're stuck trying to figure out, pick up a book and you'll tap into decades of experience. That's because the person writing the book had to either do the research or go through the events he or she writes about. Here's the problem though. If you're like I used to be, the thought of sitting down to read a book makes you want to yawn.

Plus, you're so busy, when do you have time to read? Fortunately, you don't have to torture yourself to become a lifelong learner. The technology and platforms available make it easier to learn and read than probably ever before in history. Here are a few of my suggestions to help you:

Get a subscription to *Audible* and download some good books to listen to while you're traveling on the road, working out, or whenever you have time. At the time I'm writing this book I don't have an *Audible* account, but I know so many people who do and love it! Audible is a paid subscription-based platform. I've found that most of the audiobooks I would have to pay for on Audible are available for free through my library. Check with your local library to see if they have something you can take advantage of.

Open an account for *Hoopla, RBDigital, or OverDrive* account at your library. These platforms are free and allow you to check out several eBooks and audiobooks each month. Some platforms will even let you download free movies. If you want to go this route, get a library card, create a login for the platform your library offers, and start checking out books.

After a while, you'll have your own personal library of favorite books you've read. I believe that a man with no library is a man who lacks wisdom. In the past four years, I've easily read over 300 books. Since I've started reading more, I've tried things that have made positive impacts on almost every area of my own life.

I want to encourage you to start building your own collection of books, courses, podcasts, apps, blogs, companies, community groups, businesses, and anything else you can think of that you or someone you know might be able to benefit from. For me, learning isn't fun if I can't read what I'm interested in. This isn't high school or college.

You can read whatever you want now. Choose to read and learn about things that will add value to your life. This is my approach. I have several categories I'm interested in reading about. I switch between the categories in whatever order I feel like, but the main thing is that I'm always working to learn how to improve in these areas. Your categories might be completely different—and that's fine—just take the time to invest in learning and growing.

Here's an example of the categories that I switch between reading:

- Spiritual growth

- Marriage

- Parenting

- Communication Skills

- Business

- Personal Development (exercise, a hobby, etc.).

90

WORK FROM YOUR STRENGTHS—
WORK ON YOUR WEAKNESSES

Work *from* your strengths. Work *on* your weaknesses. Let's say you're a point guard and the strongest part of your game is a layup. When you step onto the floor, you're going to focus your energy on making the most layups possible. You know your three-point shot is a little weak, so you work on it during practice to become a well-rounded player.

The same holds true in life. You *should* be operating in those areas where you're most gifted and talented. Just be sure to work on areas that need improvement as well. For instance, you might be great at doing technical jobs and work as a computer engineer, but you decide to join *Toastmasters* because you need to improve your social skills and ability to speak in front of other people.

Working on your strengths and never working on your weaknesses is like working out one bicep but never the other. It creates an imbalance. Find ways to continually grow in multiple areas of your life.

91

MYTHS ABOUT MANHOOD

You're not black. I'm allowing you to have a free bag of rice and you won't take it?" I'll never forget this interesting encounter I had at the grocery store. That day I had several bags of rice in my shopping cart and the clerk skipped one of them as she was ringing them up. After I brought it to her attention, she whispered, "Don't worry about it. You don't have to pay for it."

After I refused her offer several times, she rolled her eyes and seemed disgusted by the fact that I wasn't looking for a free handout. To her, this meant that I wasn't true to my ethnicity. And just for the record, she was a black woman herself. Like her myth about what it means to be black, there are myths about what it means to be a "real man" that are just as ridiculous. Unfortunately, most men at some point buy into these types of silly ideas.

They believe the false notions that how many beers you can chug down or how well you can withstand hard liquor are what makes you a man. Others believe that successfully getting a woman to sleep with them equates to manliness. And even worse, the false idea that sleeping with a lot of women is somehow the mark of a real man. If you've believed these types of lies, don't be fooled. Your call to manhood is much higher than this.

Choose to be a different kind of man. Not the kind who thinks that the louder and more frequently you can use "f-bombs," the more masculine you sound. Too many men settle for a cheap version of manhood that's based on how much respect you can get from others rather than by living by the right principles.

"Just because you have a plunger, it doesn't mean you're a plumber!" These were the words of my fourth-grade P.E. teacher. He went on to explain that chasing after women isn't what makes you a man. "Just because you can get a woman pregnant it doesn't mean you're a man. Just because you have a child, it doesn't mean you're a dad."

Didn't he know who he was talking to? We were a group of boys who were more interested in whether we would have pizza or tacos for lunch, or who was going to score the most touchdowns during recess. But he was smart enough to know that eventually, we would have to choose whether we would become men or stay boys.

We would have to decide whether we would play around or step up to the plate and take care of our responsibilities. I had to deal with some of these same things too, but at some point, I had to make a decision to grow up and start being a man. If you need it, this is a challenge for you to stop living out these silly myths about what it means to be a man.

Part Ten

A MAN OF FAITH

92

TURNING SELF-DOUBT INTO FAITH

With faith you can conquer your life's greatest challenges. As a man you will reach points in your life when everything inside of you will tell you it's impossible; there's no way you're going to be able to tackle this. You might have heard people say things like, "just look deep within yourself," or "you can do it, you just gotta believe in yourself."

I can understand why someone would say that, but if I had to be honest, that doesn't always work for me. The greatest strength I've ever found has come from my relationship with Christ. Jim Cymbala said one of the most humbling and difficult things any man can ever admit: "I discovered an astonishing truth: God is attracted to weakness: he cannot resist those who humbly and honestly admit how desperately they need him."

God is not only a *source* of strength, but He also shows us a great *example* of perseverance and endurance that we can gain inspiration from. Imagine having a friend you invested a lot of time into, only to have them betray you for a little bit of money. You've done a lot to help other people, but when it's your turn and you need support, none of your friends are anywhere to be found.

You go through the worse physical, mental, and emotional pain anyone could ever go through and you're in a situation that seems completely hopeless. That sounds like a horrible situation but that describes exactly what Jesus Christ went through. He knows what it's like to face the realities of a cold and dark world. All these events are recorded in the Gospels.

You might find yourself facing an uphill battle, struggling to see any way out. You might even try looking "within" to draw strength. A few months ago, my sensei had us jump over a tall stack of kicking pads as part of our training. By this point, my shirt was drenched in sweat and my lungs were burning. I thought to myself, "I'm not sure I can do this; that looks pretty high."

That's when self-doubt crept in. Just before attempting my jump, I prayed for God's strength and recited the words of one of my most often used Bible verses: "I can do all things through Christ which strengtheneth me."[45] After getting a running start, I took a "leap of faith." Once my feet left the ground it almost felt like I was flying through the air in slow motion. I cleared those pads with no problem.

Martial arts training is one of the things that tests and fortifies my faith and strength of character. Life is like that sometimes too. It can feel like things are stacked up against your favor, but those things can become opportunities to cultivate a dependence upon God, allowing Him to show you that He can empower you to do more than you ever imagined.

When it feels like *I can't*, I turn it into an *I can*, by remembering that "I can do all things through Christ which strengtheneth me."[46] My greatest strength doesn't come from turning self-doubt into self-confidence, but rather relying on God: the One who promised to be with me through whatever I go through.

He's the one who can give me the power to overcome the doubts, adversities, and struggles I face. With how crazy the world is, I couldn't even imagine what it would be like not relying on Christ as the source of my victory and strength. Each day I'm faced with the reality that there is some area I'm struggling to gain victory in. If you're honest, you probably do too. Learning to turn self-doubt into faith in what God can empower you to do is liberating.

REFLECTION QUESTIONS

1. Do you ever experience anxiety over situations that seem nearly hopeless or impossible to deal with?

2. Do you know what it's like to experience the power of Jesus in your life to help you be victorious? If so, name an instance where this happened.

3. If you've never given your life to Christ, would you be willing to find out what it takes to do so?

93

A FATHER'S FAITH

How I live impacts my children's lives. If there's anything I can pass on to my children, it would be my faith. Sometimes fathers either lack faith or do very little to pass on what they have to their children. Throughout my life, my dad struggled.

He was never the type of man who would go to church, read a Bible, or even talk about spiritual things. As I grew older, I started seeing what was missing in my dad's life all those years: he never enjoyed a personal relationship with God. As a dad, I have a tremendous impact on my children's lives.

I prefer that when my children grow up, they remember their dad praying with them, spending time with them, and being an example of a man of faith. That means that they see how I deal with struggles and rely on God's strength to help me. I give them a pattern to follow so that when they get older and encounter their own struggles, they know who to run to.

The reality is that one day their dad won't be there. I want them to have a relationship with their Heavenly Father. You might not leave your children a large inheritance, but you can give them a father's faith. To get a better understanding of the faith that I'm talking about, check out this video called, "How to Be Saved."

You can find it at https://youtu.be/JrGuzU55QOQ. They do a great job explaining things in a way that's easy to understand and the video has a great cinematic feel to it.

94

HOPE FOR THE FATHERLESS

As a child I had an unshakeable faith. My dad would tell me he was going to pick me up at a certain time. Hours beforehand I would sit at the window and many times wouldn't even eat because all I could think about was how much fun it was going to be to hang out with my dad. My mom was a great woman who never said anything negative about my dad. She would ask me if I wanted something to eat and I wouldn't move.

Every now and then I would nearly fall out of my chair as my eyes closed and my head jerked forward from being so tired. My mom ached to see me like this. But I never learned my lesson. I continued to go back to that same spot at the window each time. And most times I was disappointed. It was through those experiences I gained growing up that I decided what type of father I wanted to be to my children.

I want to be someone who's there for them and can guide them. I don't want my children sitting at the window waiting for a dad who never shows up. I've been blessed to be married for almost ten years now and my daughters have been blessed to have their dad around. But if I'm honest, even though we live under the same roof, there have been times where I've left them "sitting at the window." Times when I had "more important things" on my agenda and failed to "show up" like the way I was supposed to.

As much as I try not to, there are times where I make a promise I can't keep. I have a Heavenly Father who isn't like that. What He says He will always do. One of the greatest promises He's made me is that He won't leave me sitting by the window wondering if He will ever come for me.

I find comfort knowing that no matter how bad things get here on Earth, one day my Heavenly Father will come for me. This is what gives me a sense of hope and peace: knowing that the tragedies and difficulties I experience and witness aren't all there is.

One day I'll be able to be in Heaven with my Father. If you don't already have the peace of knowing this, I hope you'll be open to learning how you can experience the same thing. There is hope for the fatherless as well as for those who experienced less of their father than they should have.

95

YOUR SPIRITUAL HEALTH
IS IMPORTANT TOO

You can maintain good spiritual health by having a daily routine where you practice things that will help you prepare spiritually and mentally for the challenges you might experience throughout the day. The perfect time to do that is early in the mornings. This is when you can spend time reading inspirational material, doing a Bible study, praying, meditating, and reflecting on the things you're grateful for.

When a boxer steps into the ring, he has to fight his way toward victory. But how foolish would it be for him to show up right before the fight, run into the ring, and start fighting without doing a warm-up, stretching, or any other preparation? He might last a few rounds. He might even have natural talent, but he isn't giving himself the best opportunity to win.

Don't step into the "ring" every day without being prepared. If you do, you could find yourself showing up to work in a bad mood, not ready to put your best foot forward. It's easy for this to happen, especially if you're constantly rushing out of the house in the morning to try and get to work, end up having a busy day, and never have any time for reflection or taking care of your spiritual health. If you neglect your spiritual health, you're not giving yourself the best opportunity to prepare for the "fights" you will face each day. I'll include some resources you can use to help you get started. What would happen if you went weeks or months without showering?

You probably wouldn't smell too great. Likewise, what happens to your spiritual health when you neglect it? If this is not something you're used to doing, it might be difficult at first. Like anything, you can learn to develop this habit.

REFLECTION EXERCISE

1. Wake up fifteen to twenty minutes earlier than you normally do. Have a stopwatch handy and set it for 5 minutes. Read an inspirational or religious text for five minutes. Reset your stopwatch, grab a journal, and write down things you're grateful for, jot down any thoughts that come to mind. Finish the last five minutes in prayer. That fifteen-minute routine can make a big difference in your life.

2. Find 5-7 Bible verses you need to be reminded of every day. Post one on your mirror, on the fridge, next to your computer, etc. Here are the ones I chose for myself you might be able to use as well:

    -Ephesians 5:25

    -Ephesians 6:4

    -Galatians 6:9

    -Proverbs 4:23

    -Proverbs 18:21

-Taking Time to Change / Changed into His Image by Jim Berg: this is a great Bible study workbook that helps you make sense of life and makes it very easy to develop a regular habit of working on your spiritual health. I highly recommend this resource.

-Bible Hub: this is a great app that allows you to do side-by-side comparisons of different Bible versions. You can also pull up a verse of Scripture, and if you want to know more about it, just click on a button and it will pull up a ton of commentaries that will help you get a better understanding.

-Thompson Chain Reference Bible app: A great resource for helping you do Bible studies based on topics you want to focus on (ex: anger, love, etc.).

-The Bible Memory App: this is a great tool you can use to help you memorize Bible verses easier. One way you could put this to use is to try and memorize a verse from The Book of Psalms if you need encouragement.

Part Eleven

THERE'S SOMETHING DIFFERENT ABOUT HIM

96

SUCCESS BY PUTTING OTHERS FIRST

This section is all about doing the little things that make you different. Not just for the sake of standing out but because the world needs more of it. Men who don't just fall in line with being average or settling for mediocrity. When people see you, they should say to themselves, there's something different about him.

At work, in your community, there should be something that attracts people to you. The way you carry yourself, your attitude, the things that come out of your mouth. You can make a huge impact just by the little things you do. The greatest path to success is one that promotes the highest well-being of others.

This means that sometimes you might have to make decisions where you know you're going to lose something, but you do it anyway because you're not just focused on getting to the top. One year I was up for promotion and needed to complete a career advancement course before I was considered competitive enough to get the position. I enrolled in the course and got a confirmed start date.

While waiting to begin my course I was transferred to a different assignment.

Once I got there, I discovered they needed me at my new assignment more than I needed to go to that course. This put me in a dilemma: "Should I leave those who needed me and attend a course for my promotion, or should I stay and look out for them instead?"

Many of my peers told me I shouldn't worry about those under me. "Sometimes you just gotta look out for yourself," they said. While I understood their logic, they didn't quite understand that for me it was bigger than achieving personal success. I chose to stay and not attend that course, knowing it was very likely that I would be passed up for promotion.

Not completing that course was almost a guarantee that I wouldn't get selected for promotion. That year, when the promotion results came out, guess what happened? I was chosen. When everyone else said I would lose out by putting others first, I chose to do what I felt was the right thing to do. In your pursuit of success, choose to put the highest well-being of others first. It will make your success that much more fulfilling.

REFLECTION QUESTIONS

1. Do you believe it's important to put others first?

2. Do you remember a situation where someone chose to put your needs above their own self-interest of achieving success?

3. Are you willing to be different and achieve success by helping others achieve success along the way?

97

BE A GENTLEMAN ANYWAY

It sometimes seems like people are caring less about the need for gentlemen. Over the years, I've noticed more women refuse to let me hold a door open for them or insist on holding the door for me instead. Some women feel like you're treating them like they're weak and incapable by showing a nice gesture. I believe, however, that most women still appreciate a man who respects women and treats them like the queens God made them to be.

When we lose gentlemen in society, that's when you find things like an elderly woman standing, while a bus full of men are seated. This is something my grandmother never tolerated. Whenever she rode the city bus, she made young men get up for her and any other elderly woman. My grandmother was the type of woman who probably would have popped someone upside the head with her newspaper for giving her "back talk." She gave free lessons in being a gentleman to guys who didn't have a clue.

Some guys are afraid of being a gentleman because they think it might make them look weak. Have you ever seen a Marine in Dress Blues? Chances are, at some point you'll hear a "Yes sir or Yes Ma'am." He might be respectful and polite, but make no mistake about it, this same guy, if provoked can make your worst nightmare seem like a celebration. If you're a dad or have children that look up to you, you're the one who sets the example for them. Make it a good one. A gentleman is someone who will never mistreat a woman and he's certainly not abusive. Choose to be a gentleman anyway, regardless of whether it's unpopular or not.

REFLECTION QUESTIONS

1. In what ways do you display qualities of a gentleman?

2. Who in your life is watching you?

3. Would you want other people to treat your mom or sister the way you treat other women?

98

WHEN YOU GET TO THE TOP, HELP OTHERS GET THERE TOO

Is money going to change you?" This was a question one of my friends asked me with a lighthearted smile after reading a draft version of my book. I didn't answer him right away. I just stood there with my hand under my chin. My response: "I don't think so." He told me he believed in me and that he could see me making it big and influencing a lot of people with my books.

He put his hand under his chin, stared at me, and said "Naw, I don't think money would change you either." We laughed about it and then I said, "This is a question I've thought about before, and if I have a lot of money, I wouldn't want to tell the whole world anyway, so I don't think it would change me."

He got me with the famous line, "when you got money you can't hide it." My response was yeah, of course I'll probably do some renovations but I'm not planning on making any drastic lifestyle changes—except for traveling more. I explained that the same way I'm spending time to write this book to help others is the same way I would invest time to help other people if I made it big financially.

It's the same thing. It's about helping people along the way. When you get to the top, help others get there too. Use your position and influence to help lift others up. Don't ever forget you didn't start at the top and neither will those who will seek your help and support.

REFLECTION QUESTIONS

1. What things have you learned that you can share with someone else?

2. Who can you help get to the level you have reached in life? Write down the time and date you can meet with this person and areas where you can help them (spiritually, physically, etc.)

3. Do you need someone to help you get to the top? If so, write down anyone that comes to mind and commit to asking them for their support.

99

HE DOESN'T TALK BAD ABOUT PEOPLE

The same person who will tell you everyone else's business is the same person who will tell everyone else your business. This was the advice my mom gave me as a boy. She has set a great example for me because anytime she ever had someone come to her and speak negatively about another person, she always sent them away.

She never tolerated or took part in this type of behavior. I know people who have lost jobs because they chose to speak badly about management, not thinking about the consequences, and it backfired. Eleanor Roosevelt once said, "Great minds discuss ideas; average minds discuss events; small minds discuss people."

When you're dealing with a person who gossips, you'll do one of three things: listen but not say anything negative; listen and chime in with negative comments; tell the person you don't want to take part in the discussion and ask to talk about something more positive. Stay focused and concentrate on ways to build people up rather than participate in activities that tear them down.

REFLECTION QUESTIONS

1. Could you do a better job not taking part in conversations where others are engaging in gossip?

2. Out of the three types of minds quoted earlier, which one do you think more closely fits you (great mind; average mind; small mind)

3. What will you do if you find yourself in a situation where someone is speaking negatively about another person?

100

NOT AFRAID TO STEP OUT THERE

When you're starting something new it can be uncomfortable, but don't let that fear keep you from stepping out and trying something different. Successful people aren't known and appreciated for doing what most people do, but for doing what most won't. A man standing on a ledge is about to take his first step out onto a tight rope.

The only thing between him and the ground is a thin black net, and you've never seen him do this before. You probably think he's crazy for stepping out there but deep down you admire him for being willing to be so brave. When you step out into new territory, it might feel like stepping onto a tight rope several feet off the ground.

This can mean starting a new job, relocating to a new city, launching a business, but whatever it is, you can either stay where you are and fear what will happen if you don't succeed. You can also step out and attempt what could be your greatest success yet. It's time to step out there!

REFLECTION QUESTIONS

1. Is there something you want to step out there and do but you're hesitant about?

2. What things concern you the most about stepping out and moving toward your goal?

3. If you take that step and move toward your goal, what will life be like for you if things go the way you want them to?

4. What do you plan to do to make your goal a reality?

101

FINISH, FLIP, OR FAIL

When it comes to getting things done, there are three types of people: the finisher, the flipper, and the failure. There's the man that is given a task and can almost always be counted on to finish it. He doesn't get distracted by all the bells and whistles and intricate details.

This guy falls into the category of the minimalist—the person who has made it a habit of choosing the most simple way of getting things done. He's known for finishing what he starts: he's a man of action. Other men are flippers. Like someone flipping through TV channels, they go from one thing to the next.

They're men of action as well, but unfortunately, they never stick with something long enough to see whether they would fail or succeed. It would be better to find one thing to be great at than to jump from one thing to the next and never have anything to show for it.

Too many men quit before they start and an even greater number before they have a chance to see *any* type of result—good or bad. I'm not saying to stick with something that's not working just for the sake of saying you didn't give up; there's a difference between being effective and just wasting your time.

It might be fun to keep flipping because you get the thrill, but eventually, you're going to have to settle down and focus on one thing. If you're a flipper, let me give you a sage piece of advice one of my mentors gave me: "You can do everything, you just can't do everything "right now" (Denice Kennedy).

If you're trying to do everything all at once, you'll end up barely doing anything at all. If you're a man of many dreams, pick one and make it happen. The last group is those who have reached the point where they feel like a failure. This happens because they've either been "flippers" for so long with nothing to show for it, or they've just not been men of action.

They're at a point in life where they regret not doing things they feel they should have. These are the types of things that will keep you from being productive. Each of these men wants to be great but it's only the man of action—the finisher, who will look back and be able to smile at what God has blessed him to be able to accomplish. Which one will you be?

Get Free Printable Workbook & Bonus Material
www.habitsforgrowth.com/bonus101

CONCLUSION

I hope now that you've read *101 Things Every Man Should Know: To Experience a Life of Victory & Impact*, you have an even deeper commitment to bettering yourself and reaching your full potential. Some of the most life-changing things you could ever discover are buried away somewhere in a book. Because of that, I hope you will continue to read books like this that will challenge and inspire you.

Work hard, have fun, dream big. Stay focused, use your time wisely, and be consistent with doing those small habits that will pay off big for you. Use your strength to bring out the best in others and to make the world a better place. Thank you for taking the time to read this book. Much success to you!

Reviews are gold to authors:
If you've enjoyed this book, would you consider rating it and leaving a review on Amazon?

GET A **FREE** COPY!

ABC's of FINANCIAL EXCELLENCE

~~$11.99~~ Value!

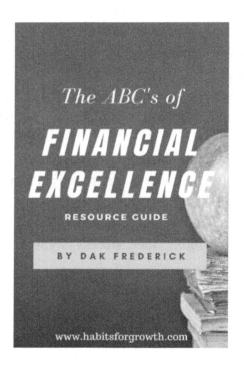

Get a free copy of this upcoming release:

www.habitsforgrowth.com/financialexcellence

ABOUT THE AUTHOR

Dak Frederick is an author, entrepreneur, and retired U.S. Marine Gunnery Sergeant. More importantly, he is happily married, a dad to two wonderful daughters, and a follower of Christ. He seeks to help men who hunger for a life of excellence and impact.

He believes that today's effort causes tomorrow's reality and that with diligence, perseverance, faith, and a passion for learning and growing, you can achieve more than you ever imagined.

He also hosts the Habits for Growth podcast, which serves as not only a resource to help you get your finances in check, but also a place where you can find inspiration by hearing other men as they share their faith and open up about their struggles and successes.

He is a musician and singer and has also been ministering alongside his wife since 2011, bringing a message of hope and encouragement through music. He and his wife launched the YouTube channel, Music and Marriage, where they sing uplifting music and have candid conversations about marriage.

Get Free Printable Workbook and Bonus Material
www.habitsforgrowth.com/bonus101

NOTES

CHAPTER 7

1.   Jim Daily, "Redeeming Fatherhood When It's Broken—Jim Daly's Story," Focus on the Family, June 19, 2020, YouTube, https://www.youtube.com/watch?v=XlaPg9dazfs.

CHAPTER 12

2.   "6 Surprising Symbiotic Relationships: Nile Crocodile and Egyptian Plover," Wildlife Woods, March 11, 2020, https://wildlifewoods.net/blog/2018/8/23/6-surprising-symbiotic-relationships.

CHAPTER 21

3.   The Art of Improvement, "A Complete Guide to Goal Setting," YouTube, November 11, 2018, https://www.youtube.com/watch?v=XpKvs-apvOs

CHAPTER 22

4.   The Editors of Encyclopaedia Britannica, "Glenn Cunningham," Encyclopedia Britannica, March 6, 2021, https://www.britannica.com/biography/Glenn-Cunningham.

5.   "How to Make a Vision Board," wikiHow, updated August 26, 2020, https://www.wikihow.com/Make-a-Vision-Board.

CHAPTER 23

6.   "Burnout" *Merriam-Webster*, https://www.merriam-webster.com/dictionary/burnout, accessed June 9, 2021.

7.   "What Does Holding a Grudge Do to Your Health?," Piedmont Healthcare, accessed June 3, 2021, https://www.piedmont.org/living-better/what-does-holding-a-grudge-do-to-your- health.

CHAPTER 25

8.   Julie Compton, "One Small Thing: Use Micro Habits to

Tackle Big Health and Productivity Goals," NBC News, June 1, 2017, https://www.nbcnews.com/better/one-smallthing/how-use-micro-habits-tackle-big-health-goals-n766691.101 Things Every Man Should Know (To Experience a Life of Victory & Impact) 212.

CHAPTER 29

9.   Henry Cloud, "Integrity: The Courage to Meet the Demands of Reality," (Harper Collins Publishers, 2006, 147-153).

CHAPTER 31

10.   Michael Hyatt and Megan Hyatt Miller, hosts, "#114: How to Make Your Vision a Reality," Lead to Win, podcast, 3:26-3:55, April 14, 2020, December 15, 2020, https://podcasts.apple.com/us/podcast/lead-to-win/id1294885433?i=1000471421566.

11.   Michael Hyatt and Megan Hyatt Miller, Make Your Vision a Reality.

CHAPTER 41

12.   Alex Kendrick, director, Courageous, (Sherwood Pictures, 2011).

CHAPTER 51

13.   "Benefits of Community Service," Community Engagement, Western Connecticut State University, accessed June 3, 2021, www.wcsu.edu/community-engagement/benefits-of-volunteering/#:~:text=Volunteering%20increases%20self%2Dconfidence.,sense%20of%20pride%20and%20identity.

CHAPTER 53

14.   Gregg Fidan, "How Much Can You Save Buying a Used Car?," accessed June 3, 2021, https://www.realcartips.com/usedcars/414-saving-money-used-car.shtml#:~:text=With%20an%20average%20selling%20price,about%20%20%244%2C000%20in%20depreciation%20costs.

15.   Ramit Sethi, "Should I buy a new car or used car?," April 15, 2020, https://www.iwillteachyoutoberich.com/blog/cost-vs-value-

should-you-buy-a-new-car-or-used-car.

CHAPTER 55

16 "Budgeting: How to create a budget and stick with it," Consumer Finance Protection Bureau, accessed June 9, 2021, https://www.consumerfinance.gov/about-us/blog/budgeting-how-to-create-a-budget-and-stick-with-it/.

CHAPTER 56

17.   Dacher Keltner and Jason Marsh, "How Gratitude Beats Materialism," Greater Good Magazine, January 8, 2015, https://greatergood.berkeley.edu/article/item/materialism_gratitude_happiness.

18.   "Materialism," Merriam-Webster, www.merriam-webster.com/dictionary/materialism, accessed June 9, 2021.

CHAPTER 60

19.   10 Leading Causes of Death, United States 2019, All Races, Both Sexes," National Center for Injury Prevention and Control, Centers for Disease Control and Prevention, accessed June 9, 2021, https://webappa.cdc.gov/cgi-bin/ broker .exe? _service=v8prod&_server=aspv-wisq-1.cdc.gov&_port=5099&_sessionid=D8QVJO0tQ52&_program=wisqars.dd_leadcaus10.sas&log=1&rept=&State=00&year1=2019&year2=2019&Race=0&Ethnicty=0&Sex=0&ranking=10&PRTF MT=FRIENDLY&lcdfmt=lcd1age&category=ALL&c_age1=0&c_age2=0&_debug=0

CHAPTER 64

20.   Jendayi Harris, The Chubby Church: A Call to Break Free of Weight and Eating Bondage, book 1, (Whole & Free Press, 2019, 102).

21.   "Water IS Life, Drink Up!," Nourished, August 1, 2018, https://nourished.com/water-is-life-drink-up.

22.   "The Importance of Hydration," News, Harvard T.H. Chan, School of Public Health, accessed June 3, 2021, www.hsph.harvard.edu/news/hsph-in-the-news/the-importance-of-

hydration.

23.   Joseph Mercola, "How Much Water Should I Drink?," accessed May 20, 2021, https://articles.mercola.com/how-much-water-should-i-drink.aspx.

CHAPTER 65

24.   Dr. Josh Axe, "Benefits of Intermittent Fasting + How to Do It," Ancient Medicine Today, August 3, 2017, YouTube, https://www.youtube.com/watch?v=8xv2cWhnkPU.

25.   Rachel Link, "Intermittent Fasting: A Beginner's Guide to Improving Health and Losing Weight," Dr. Axe, May 16, 2018, https://draxe.com/nutrition/intermittent-fasting-benefits.

CHAPTER 66

26.   Water Science School, "The Water in You: Water and the Human Body," U.S. Geological Survey (USGS), accessed June 10, 2021, https://www.usgs.gov/special-topic/water-science-school/science/water-you-water-and-human-body?qt-science_center_objects=0#qt-science_center_objects.

27.   Donald Colbert, The Seven Pillars of Health, (Siloam, 2006).

CHAPTER 68

28.   Hilary Parker, "A sweet problem: Princeton researchers find that high-fructose corn syrup prompts considerably more weight gain," Princeton University, March 22, 2010, https://www.princeton.edu/news/2010/03/22/sweet-problem-princeton-researchers-find-high-fructose-corn-syrup-prompts.

29.   Hilary Parker, "A sweet problem."

30.   Josh Axe, "High Fructose Corn Syrup Dangers and Healthy Alternatives," Dr. Axe, April 2, 2021, https://draxe.com/nutrition/high-fructose-corn-syrup-dangers/.

31.   Phys.org, "Structuring sweetness: What makes Stevia 200 times sweeter than sugar, June 10, 2019," https://phys.org/news/2019-06-sweetness-stevia-sweeter-sugar.html.

32.   Marjan Ajami et al., "Effects of stevia on glycemic and lipid

profile of type 2 diabetic patients: A randomized controlled trial, "Avicenna journal of phytomedicine," 10, no. 2 (2020): 118-127, https://www.ncbi.nlm.nih.gov/pmc/articles/PMC7103435/.

CHAPTER 69
33. Shawn Stevenson, "Sleep Smarter: 21 Proven Tips to Sleep Your Way to a Better Body, Better Health, and Bigger Success," (Harmony/Rodale, 2016, 2).

34. Suni, Eric, "What Causes Insomnia," accessed June 7, 2021, https://www.sleepfoundation.org/insomnia/what-causes-insomnia#:~:text=Common%20causes%20of%20insomnia%20include,problems%2C%20and%20specific%20sleep%20disorders.

CHAPTER 70
35. Jillian Levy, "6 Steps to Get Your Cortisol Levels Under Control & Turn Down the Stress," Dr. Axe, updated June 14, 2018, https://draxe.com/health/cortisol-levels/.

36. Jillian Levy, "Get Your Cortisol Levels Under Control."

CHAPTER 71
37. "National Diabetes Statistics Report," Centers for Disease Control and Prevention, last updated August 28, 2020, accessed June 9, 2021, https://www.cdc.gov/diabetes/data/statistics-report/index.html.

38 "The Role of Vitamin D in Preventing Type 2 Diabetes," Grassroots Health Nutrient Research Institute, accessed June 7, 2021, https://www.grassrootshealth.net/blog/role-vitamin-d-preventing-type-2-diabetes.

CHAPTER 73
39 Libby Sander, "The Case for Finally Cleaning Your Desk," Harvard Business Review, March 25, 2019, https://hbr.org/2019/03/the-case-for-finally-cleaning-your-desk.

CHAPTER 79
41 George Thompson and Jerry Jenkins, "Verbal Judo: The Gentle Art of Persuasion," (Harper Collins Publishers, 2013).

CHAPTER 83

CHAPTER 92

Made in the USA
Middletown, DE
13 July 2021